WHAT EVERY TEEN SHOULD KNOW
ABOUT TEXAS LAW

WHAT *Every* TEEN SHOULD KNOW ABOUT *Texas Law*

L. JEAN WALLACE
CHRISTOPHER F. CYPERT

UNIVERSITY OF TEXAS PRESS ❧ AUSTIN

Requests for permission to reproduce material
from this work should be sent to:
Permissions
University of Texas Press
P.O. Box 7819
Austin, TX 78713-7819
utpress.utexas.edu/rp-form

The paper used in this book meets the minimum requirements of
ANSI/NISO Z39.48–1992 (R1997) (Permanence of Paper). ♾

Book design by Lindsay Starr
Typesetting by BookComp, Inc.

Library of Congress Cataloging-in-Publication Data

Names: Wallace, L. Jean (Lily Jean), 1951– author. | Cypert, Christopher F.,
author.
Title: What every teen should know about Texas law / L. Jean Wallace,
Christopher F. Cypert.
Other titles: What every 18-year-old needs to know about Texas law
Description: Third edition. | Austin : University of Texas Press, 2018. |
Includes index.
Identifiers: LCCN 2017046027
ISBN 978-1-4773-1563-7 (pbk. : alk. paper)
ISBN 978-1-4773-1565-1 (library e-book)
ISBN 978-1-4773-1566-8 (non-library e-book)
Subjects: LCSH: Law--Texas--Juvenile literature. | Teenagers—Legal status,
laws, etc.—Texas—Juvenile literature.
Classification: LCC KFT1281 .W28 2018 | DDC 349.764—dc23
LC record available at https://lccn.loc.gov/2017046027

doi:10.7560/315644

A special thank you to Ms. L. Jean Wallace for allowing me to revise and rewrite this book. It has been a pleasure.

Rules to Live By

———

1. Life is not fair.

2. What you do today will affect you tomorrow.

3. There is no such thing as a free lunch.

4. Ignorance of the law is no excuse.

5. Follow the Golden Rule: do unto others as you would have them do unto you.

6. Ask questions.

7. Never sign anything if you don't know what you are signing.

8. The more you know, the less threatened you will feel.

CONTENTS

5. Personal Relationships, 112

6. Employment and Consumer Concerns and Other Issues, 131

7. Living on Your Own, 148

8. How to Do It Yourself, 185

INTRODUCTION

You are almost there, and, I bet, you can actually begin to see the light at the end of your high-school tunnel. I'm sure, like most people your age, you believe that light to represent adulthood and freedom. And you would be correct. However, with age comes more and more responsibility. Violation of these responsibilities can sometimes have serious penalties that may not be apparent to you at the time of the action.

The purpose of *What Every Teen Should Know about Texas Law* is to acquaint you with the broad range of basic rights you have, responsibilities you possess, and penalties that you may incur. In January 2011, David Ropeik wrote an article published in *Psychology Today* titled: "Why Do We Keep Predicting the Future if We Are So Often Wrong?" In this article he states, "Human beings always have and always will try to predict the future to give themselves a feeling of control," claiming that "the less people know, the more threatened they feel." With those two statements in mind, this book has been filled with information so that you may know, before you act. As an elected municipal judge for the past seventeen years in a northern Texas city, I have seen young people make decisions that have stunted their dreams and crushed their goals. One night out with your friends can dramatically affect the plans you have for the rest of your life. In revising this book, I hope to calm any fears you may have, share a little insight concerning your transition to adulthood, and provide you some control over your future. I hope to peak your interest just enough that you may devise a plan on how you will respond when confronted with some of the topics discussed here.

I have arranged this text in an order that will benefit you as you get closer to adulthood. In case you haven't already taken a driver's education course and received your driver's license, we will begin with the steps of how to do it. We will discuss the process of traffic stops, your rights if you are ever questioned by a police officer, the procedures of court, and what jail is really like. (It stinks, both literally and emotionally.) Laws regarding personal relationships, jobs, your credit, and living on your own are outlined in the following chapters. A few of these chapters may seem of little interest to you now. Nevertheless, I have found, most people need a little help the first time, and should be aware of the law, as they sign a lease for an apartment, experience their first traffic accident, decide to get married, or should they need to make a complaint against, or even compliment, a police officer.

Some of the laws or processes discussed may seem unnecessary or even unfair to you, but they are what they are. As you read, keep in mind I do not share how I think laws should be interpreted or even if some of them should be changed. That is not the purpose of this book. There is a section in chapter 8 on how *you* can change them though. You can get involved. You may decide, as young as sixteen, to serve as a student election clerk, or when you turn eighteen, you may want to register to vote. Some of you may even choose to run for political office, but, no matter at what level, each of us can, and probably should, be involved in some way in our Texas political process.

The information included is general and intended for your information purposes only. DO NOT accept this as legal advice. If you have a specific legal problem, you should always seek advice from an attorney. Remember, the laws discussed are for Texas only. Laws in other states may be, and usually are, very different. The information included is regarding current law at the time of writing. Because laws change constantly, in a very few instances, the law as quoted may no longer be accurate.

You will also see that periodically inserted in the text is a story to illustrate the material. These stories are true, but they did not all happen to one unfortunate family. Some of these stories I have experienced in my time on the bench. Others come from Ms. L. Jean Wallace, the original author who provided the bones for this work. She heard them while serving in her capacity as attorney for students at Texas Tech University. While some of the stories may be amusing, our hope is you will not miss the point.

WHAT EVERY TEEN SHOULD KNOW
ABOUT TEXAS LAW

Chapter 1

THE CONSTITUTION OF
THE UNITED STATES

The Constitution of the United States is the very foundation of the laws that govern and protect us all. The next few pages are not meant to be a history lesson; however, I think they are the only way to begin a book on the topic of the rights we possess.

The United States Constitution is the supreme law of the land for the United States of America. The Constitution was originally made up of seven "articles" that provide for the framework of our government. The first three articles explain the separation of powers, dividing the federal government into three branches: the executive, consisting of the president; the legislative, consisting of both houses of Congress (Senate and House of Representatives); and the judicial, consisting of the Supreme Court and other federal courts. The Constitution also explains the responsibilities of each of these three branches. Congress is given authority to create law, the court's job is to interpret the law, and the president is required to enforce the law.

Special Note: You have probably never thought about it this way, but I want you to realize all government follows this example. All the way down to your local government. Your city council creates local ordinances (local laws and rules). Your local courts interpret ordinances and state law. And your mayor, because the local police department works for your city, enforces all laws.

The Constitution came into effect in 1789, and has been amended (changed or added to) twenty-seven times to meet the needs of our changing nation. These changes are called "amendments." The first ten amendments, known as the "Bill of Rights," is mainly what we will discuss in the following chapters. The Bill of Rights lays out specific protections of individual liberty (freedom or rights) and justice (impartiality or fairness). It also places restrictions on the government's power over citizens.

Even though we will not be discussing the last seventeen amendments, you need to realize the majority of them were added to expand, or build upon, individual civil rights and protections (two examples: no more slavery and the right to vote for *all* citizens), while others address issues related to government authority or explain government process and procedures.

Whether you believe in God or not, the writers of the Constitution did, and they used those beliefs to build the very framework of our country. I recommend you get a copy of *our* Constitution. Read it, learn it, and always remember the first three words are "We the People." The creation and authority of the United States is only found in "We." "We the People of the United States"! This very important document explains why our country was founded and reminds us that the government of the United States exists only to serve us, its citizens.

Preamble (Introduction)

We the People of the United States, in Order to form a more perfect Union, establish Justice, insure domestic Tranquility, provide for the common defence, promote the general Welfare, and secure the Blessings of Liberty to ourselves and our Posterity, do ordain and establish this Constitution for the United States of America.

Bill of Rights

Protections of Liberty

AMENDMENT 1

Congress shall make no law respecting an establishment of religion, or prohibiting the free exercise thereof; or abridging the freedom of speech, or of the press; or the right of the people peaceably to assemble, and to petition the government for a redress of grievances.

The First Amendment prohibits Congress from obstructing the exercise of certain individual freedoms: freedom of religion, freedom of speech, freedom of the press, freedom of assembly, and the right to petition. This amendment guarantees your right to hold whatever religious belief you choose, and to freely exercise that belief. It prevents the federal government from creating an official national church or favoring one set of religious beliefs over any other. The amendment guarantees your right to express and to be exposed to a wide range of opinions and views. It was intended to ensure a free exchange of ideas even if the ideas are unpopular. It also guarantees an individual's right to physically gather, *peaceably*, with a group of people to picket or protest or associate with others in groups for economic, political, or religious purposes. Additionally, it guarantees an individual's right to petition the government for a redress of grievances (to address and fix our complaints).

AMENDMENT 2

A well-regulated militia, being necessary to the security of a free state, the right of the people to keep and bear arms, shall not be infringed.

The Second Amendment protects your right as an individual to keep and bear arms. As you will read in a later chapter, this doesn't mean certain rules don't apply. The government may regulate or place some limits on the manufacture or who can own or sell a firearm or other weapons.

Protections of Justice

AMENDMENT 4

The right of the people to be secure in their persons, houses, papers and effects, against unreasonable searches and seizures, shall not be violated, and no warrants shall issue, but upon probable cause, supported by oath or affirmation, and particularly describing the place to be searched, and the persons or things to be seized.

The Fourth Amendment protects you against unreasonable searches and seizures of either yourself or your property by government officials. A search can mean everything from a frisk by a police officer to a search of your home or car to a demand for a blood test. A seizure occurs when the government takes control of you, by arrest, or something you have in your possession. Items that are seized often are used as evidence when the individual is charged with a crime. It also imposes certain limitations on police investigating a crime and prevents them from using those items at trial if they were illegally obtained.

AMENDMENT 5

No person shall be held to answer for a capital, or otherwise infamous crime, unless on a presentment or indictment of a grand jury, except in cases arising in the land or naval forces, or in the militia, when in actual service in time of war or public danger; nor shall any person be subject for the same offense to be twice put in jeopardy of life or limb; nor shall be compelled in any criminal case to be a witness against himself, nor be deprived of life, liberty, or property, without due process of law; nor shall private property be taken for public use, without just compensation.

The Fifth Amendment creates the requirement that a trial for a major crime may only happen after an indictment has been handed down by a grand jury. It holds that all people are presumed to be innocent until *proven* guilty. It prevents you from double jeopardy: having to go to court and being put in danger of punishment more than once for the same crime. It prohibits punishment without due process of law, meaning it protects you from being imprisoned without a fair trial, and the Fifth Amendment provides that if you are accused of a crime you cannot be forced to reveal any information to the police, prosecutor, judge, or jury that may be used against you in a court of law (you don't have to testify against yourself). Additionally, the Fifth Amendment prohibits the government from taking any private property for public use without making just compensation.

AMENDMENT 6

In all criminal prosecutions, the accused shall enjoy the right to a speedy and public trial, by an impartial jury of the state and district wherein the crime shall have been committed, which district shall have been previously ascertained by law, and to be informed of the nature and cause of the accusation; to be confronted with the witnesses against him; to have compulsory process for obtaining witnesses in his favor, and to have the assistance of counsel for his defense.

I don't know why, all of a sudden, the Sixth Amendment changes the words used from "the People" to the pronouns "him" and "his," but this amendment provides several protections and rights to all individuals (man, woman, boy, or girl) accused of a crime. If accused of a crime, you have the right to a fair and speedy trial by a local and impartial jury. It provides for all court to be open court (open to the public). This protects defendants from secret proceedings that may encourage abuse of the justice system, and keeps the public informed. The Sixth Amendment guarantees a right to have legal counsel (attorney or lawyer) and gives you the right to call witnesses, to testify on your behalf, and to be told what crime you have been charged with. This amendment is what requires the "Miranda warning" that will be discussed in section § 4.1.

AMENDMENT 7

In suits at common law, where the value in controversy shall exceed twenty dollars, the right of trial by jury shall be preserved, and no fact tried by a jury, shall be otherwise reexamined in any court of the United States, than according to the rules of the common law.

The only reason I have added this one is to explain that this amendment guarantees the right to a jury trial only in federal court cases, not in all state court cases. In chapter 4, we will discuss the differences.

AMENDMENT 8

Excessive bail shall not be required, nor excessive fines imposed, nor cruel and unusual punishments inflicted.

The Eighth Amendment protects you from having bail or fines assessed at an amount so high that it would be impossible for you to pay it. It protects you from cruel and unusual punishment. Although this was originally intended to abolish certain gruesome methods of punishment, it has been broadened to protect you against punishments that are too harsh or extreme for particular crimes.

Unenumerated Rights and Reserved Powers

AMENDMENT 9

The enumeration in the Constitution, of certain rights, shall not be construed to deny or disparage others retained by the people.

This is a weird one. The Ninth Amendment declares that each individual has *other* fundamental rights, in addition to those stated in the Constitution. In the year 1791, a group argued that if "some" rights are listed, in the constitution, and not "all" it would infer that those were the "only" rights of America's citizens. They argued with another group that said "it was impossible to list every fundamental right." So the Ninth Amendment was added as a compromise. Because the rights protected by the Ninth Amendment are not specified, they are referred to as "unenumerated." The Supreme Court has found that unenumerated rights include such important rights as the right to travel, the right to vote, the right to keep personal matters private and to make important decisions about one's health care or body.

AMENDMENT 10

The powers not delegated to the United States by the Constitution, nor prohibited by it to the states, are reserved to the states respectively, or to the people.

The Tenth Amendment states that the federal government has only those powers specifically granted by the Constitution. These powers include the power to declare war, to collect taxes, to regulate interstate business activities, and others that are listed in the articles or in the amendments. Any power not listed, says the Tenth Amendment, is left to the states or the people. While there is no specific list of what these "reserved powers" may be, the Supreme Court has ruled that laws affecting family relations, commerce that occurs within a state's own borders, and local law enforcement activities, are among those specifically reserved to the states or the people. This refers to the difference in the laws from state to state.

Chapter 2

—

DRIVE TO SURVIVE

Texas has been referred to by many as a "Drive to Survive State." What is meant by this is we live in such a big and sprawling state that if you don't drive it may actually be difficult to survive. Many of our rural areas, smaller cities and towns don't have organized mass transit or even a taxicab service. Yet we must still get to work, to the doctor, and to the grocery store, and sometimes, walking or a bike simply won't get us there. People must drive to survive, but that doesn't mean that it's okay to break the law or that you won't be stopped, ticketed, or even arrested. This chapter will help you devise a plan to earn and keep the privilege of driving.

I would hope by now you have already obtained or are working diligently to get your driver's license from the Texas Department of Public Safety (DPS). If not, we may as well start with what it takes. While this process may not be as quick and easy as it is for adult applicants, you don't need to worry. The process is actually much simpler than many of you may expect it to be.

The Graduated Driver License Program

2.1. The Process

Any prospective driver *under the age of 21* in our state must go through the Graduated Driver License Program (GDL Program). This program makes sure each person learning to drive will go through different phases of driving "privileges" before earning a full unrestricted license. These phases exist because driving is an earned privilege, not a right, with incredible responsibilities.

You may as well start now because you must fulfill the following time requirements in order to earn each respective phase of the GDL:

Learner's permit—at least fifteen years old with six of thirty-two hours of driver's education completed.
Intermediate license—six months after holding a learner's license.
Provisional license—one year after holding an intermediate license without any road violations.
Unrestricted license—when a provisional license holder turns eighteen years old without any major violations.

You did notice all the "without violations" clauses, right?

2.2. Learner's Permit

If you want to drive, you can start a driver's education course as soon as you turn fourteen years old but must wait until you are fifteen to be eligible for a leaner's permit. The driver's education course typically consists of thirty-two hours of classroom instruction and forty-four hours of behind-the-wheel training. Once achieved the learner's permit will allow you the ability to drive a vehicle with the sole purpose of learning to drive. You will be required at *all times* to drive with a licensed passenger (front passenger) aged twenty-one or older. In order to be eligible, you must complete at least the first six hours of the thirty-two-hour, Texas-approved driver's education course. Once this requirement is met, you may go to your local Driver License Office and apply.

When you go to apply make sure you take the following:

1. Proof of driver's education completion of at least six hours (Texas Driver Education Certificate: form DE-964).
2. A completed application for a driver's license (form DL-14A), including a parent or guardian's signature. (Get this online or at the Driver License Office.)
3. Verification of enrollment and attendance in high school. (Hope you have always been nice to those secretaries at your school and aren't in violation of the Failure to Attend School laws.) Your high school diploma or GED will work too.
4. Two forms of proof verifying Texas residency (that form from the school will work as one).
5. Proof of identity (a certified birth certificate and a school badge with picture may work).
6. Your social security card or any proof of your social security number. (For example, a paycheck with your full social security number—will work. A paycheck with only the last four numbers will NOT.)
7. Any required fees or payment.

After you have presented these documents, you will be required to pass a DPS knowledge test. This is a forty-question, multiple-choice exam covering basic road signs and road rules. Seventy percent or better is passing.

Special Note: If you would like to obtain a Texas Identification Card (Texas ID), you will need all of the above except number 1. If there is some reason you are unable or uninterested in getting your DL, you should seriously consider getting an ID. It can be used to not only identify you but also some sort of ID is always needed to do things like cash your paychecks, vote, or open a bank account.

2.3. Intermediate License

In order to achieve your intermediate license, you must have held your learner's permit for six months without incident and completed thirty practice hours of driving, at least ten of which were done at night. The thirty hours must include at least seven hours in-car driving and seven hours in-car driving observation. Additionally, before taking the behind-the-wheel exam, you must complete the free Texas DPS Impact Texas Teen Drivers course (ITTD). Once you have completed it, you will be emailed a certificate that must be taken to DPS within ninety days. You will then be able to take the road test to apply and achieve your intermediate license.

An intermediate license will allow you the ability to drive without supervision from a licensed driver. However, there are restrictions involved for driving under this license. For the first year with this type of license, you will NOT be allowed to:

- Drive between midnight and 5 a.m. without a licensed older driver.
- Drive with more than one passenger under twenty-one years old who is not a family member.
- Drive with a wireless communication device, regardless if it is hands-free or not.

2.4. Provisional License

If you are able to drive on this intermediate license for one year without any road violations, your license will transition to a provisional license. Once you turn eighteen years old, your license will automatically be upgraded to a full unrestricted Texas driver's license.

2.5. Texas Driver's Education Course

That whole Graduated Driver License Program we just discussed begins with a driver's education program (driver's ed.). This course may be online or in a classroom, taught by an instructor or your parent, but the required hours of each class is determined by Texas state law.

- An approved written "in-classroom" course with at least thirty-two hours of instruction.
- An approved "in-car" training course that consists of at least seven hours of behind-the-wheel training and seven hours of in-car observation.
- At least thirty hours of additional behind-the-wheel training (including ten at night) supervised by a licensed parent, guardian, or instructor.

Your driver's education program may be completed in several different ways. Your options range in price and convenience, so you may want to pay close attention to the following section and, when ready, shop around.

2.6. Parent-Taught Driver's Education

The cheapest but sometimes most difficult is a "full" parent-taught program. You will need to go to the Texas Department of Licensing and Regulation website www.tdlr.texas.gov/ParentTaught and request the "NEW Parent Driver Education Guide." Once the application is completed and a required twenty-dollar fee is paid, the packet will be mailed (in one to two weeks) or emailed (in twelve to twenty-four hours) to your instructor.

Your instructor must meet certain criteria to be your instructor. He or she must be a licensed driver and be your:

- Parent;
- Stepparent;
- Grandparent;
- Step-Grandparent;
- Foster parent or
- Legal guardian appointed by a court of competent jurisdiction (for example, young people in the care of Child Protective Services).

- A Power of Attorney is NOT legally sufficient and will not work.

See *Special Note* at the end of § 2.7 for other instructor options.

2.7. Requirements for Instructor

Finding an instructor is where I have seen the majority of young people held up in this process. The requirements for the instructor state something that may make it a bit difficult for you as well. They are: *the instructor must have a valid driver's license for the preceding three years.* . . . So, if your parent is going to teach the course and his or her own driver's license was suspended, revoked, or expired, at any point, within the last three years, your parent is disqualified. He or she may check his or her own driving record for a small fee at www.texas.gov by clicking on "Driver Records," or by calling (512) 424-2600. Tell your parent not to call, though, because the phone number is rarely answered; however, if necessary, it will not hurt to try.

Other instructor restrictions include that the instructor cannot:

- Have been convicted (including a probated sentence) of Criminally Negligent Homicide;
- Have been convicted (including a probated sentence) for Driving While Intoxicated (DWI);
- Have his or her license suspended, revoked, or forfeited for traffic-related violations in the past three years;
- Have six or more points assigned to his or her driver's license (see § 2.16 for information on surcharges and points).

The instructor is responsible for checking both their criminal and driving records to verify that they are not disqualified to be a driving instructor. If your instructor fails to do so, and he or she teaches you a section of the driver's education course when he or she is not qualified, it will NOT count. You will have to complete that section again.

Special Note: As I complete this section House Bill 912 has been passed by our state legislators and signed into law by our governor. This bill changes the law and allows your parent, or legal guardian, to designate an "individual," who is at least twenty-five years old, has at least seven years of driving experience, and does not charge a fee, to teach both the classroom and driving sections of driver's ed. to you. Your parent must designate this individual on a specific form you will get from DPS. (The specific form, to be used, has not been created by Texas Department of Licensing and Regulation at the time of this writing.) The instructor must still meet the qualifications listed in § 2.7. The only difference is the instructor will NOT have to be related to you as listed in § 2.6.

2.8. Driving Instructor While in Active Military

If your instructor is active-military personnel or the spouse of someone who is, he or she must have a valid driver's license from his or her state of permanent residency or last duty station for the proceeding three years.

2.9. "Classroom" Section of Driver's Ed.

If for one reason or another, you do not believe you can be around your parents for the full seventy-six hours, or you are one of those young people who wants to do as much as possible on your own, you have the option to break up the course.

There are several online programs that will allow you to split up the course. For about one hundred dollars, you may take the classroom section without the aid of a parent, guardian, or instructor. After enrolling, and paying, you may immediately begin online. Every bit of the thirty-two-hour classroom section will be completed online and at your own pace. After completing the first six hours, the Texas Driver Education Certificate (DE-964) will be mailed or emailed to you by the online company.

If you are one of those people who learns best or wants to go to an actual classroom and have a real-life instructor, you can do that too. This type of course usually costs a bit more and has set times and dates for the classes. Make sure your schedule will accommodate these classes.

No matter which of the two options above you choose, you will still need all the forms in § 2.2 and your parent or guardian to go with you and sign off on your paperwork at the Driver License Office.

2.10. "Driving" Section of Driver's Ed.

Okay, you have the learner's permit and you have completed, or are close to completion on, the classroom section. It's time to start driving. If your chosen instructor is qualified, use him or her if they are willing. This will be the cheapest option. If your instructor is disqualified due to one of the reasons listed in § 2.7, or you don't have an "individual" your parents can designate to teach you, your only option is the traditional driver's ed. The best place to find one, you guessed it, is online. Search for driver's education programs in your area and look on their websites. This will be listed as "driving section only" or "behind-the-wheel training." This can be costly, so make sure you shop around.

Remember, if you're younger than eighteen years old, you'll need to complete a total of forty-four hours of behind-the-wheel training, including:

- Seven hours of behind-the-wheel driver's training with your driving instructor;
- Seven hours of in-car observation as part of your driver's training;
- Thirty hours of supervised practice with a licensed adult.

Now you have a driver's license. Let's talk about keeping it.

2.11. In Case You've Forgotten, Some Basic Traffic Rules

1. Everyone in the vehicle must have on a seat belt.
2. The use of a handheld device in a school zone in Texas is illegal. A lot of cities have an ordinance about NOT using a handheld device while driving at all. In a special session of

our Texas legislature, they are discussing a complete ban on texting while driving for all drivers as I type.

3. Stop signs mean a complete, dead stop. (Bicycle or motorcycle: that means one foot on the ground.)
4. If making a right turn on a red light, stop completely before making the turn.
5. Backing cars ALWAYS yield to any oncoming traffic.

Driver's License

Special Note: For the remainder of this book the commonly used word "ticket" will be used in place of the legal term "citation."

2.12. Address

You should keep your current permanent address on your driver's license at all times. Remember, this means if you move, you must go in to the local DPS office to change your address on the license. You have thirty days to do so. Failure to do so can result in a ticket with a fine of up to $200 for "Failure to Report Change of Address." If you do get a ticket for this charge, go ahead and get your license updated and provide proof to the court within the time limit the court has provided. If you do so, this charge may be dismissed with a twenty-dollar dismissal fee.

Special Note TO COLLEGE STUDENTS: If you live in the dorm or in an apartment and are not self-supporting or married, this is usually considered a temporary address, and your license need not be changed. You can keep your permanent home address on it.

It is very important to keep this address current because any notification from the DPS is sent to the address on your license. If your license is going to be suspended, you want to know about it. If away at college, alert your parent or guardian to forward any mail from DPS or any government entity (such as the tiny little town where you got that unpaid speeding ticket two months ago). Legally, if the mail was sent to the address on your license, you are deemed to have gotten notice whether you actually received it or not. Mail from DPS is not forwarded by the postal service. If DPS mails something to you and you do not live there, the post office will return the mail to DPS. If DPS receives the mail back, they know you don't live at the address you have on your license and your driving privileges are instantly suspended.

2.13. Displaying Your License

If you are stopped by an officer for any reason, you will be asked to show your license. If you fail to do so, you will be given a ticket, or may even be arrested, for "Failure to Display a Driver's License." This offense carries a fine of up to $200. If you don't have your valid license with you at the time you are ticketed, don't panic. You can get the "Failure to Display a Driver's License" charge dismissed by showing your license to the court named on the ticket within the time allowed.

2.14. Suspension of License

Listed below are various reasons for a license to be suspended. The suspension is for up to one year unless noted otherwise.

1. Habitual Violator: you receive four moving violations within twelve months or seven within twenty-four months, arising out of different incidents (two tickets issued in the same incident count as one; for a PROVISIONAL LICENSE holder, the limit is two or more moving violations within twelve months).

2. Injury in an accident: you are responsible for an accident resulting in death, serious personal injury, or serious property damage.

3. Driving while your license is suspended: If your license is already suspended and you have been convicted at least once before and are caught driving, this charge is a Class B misdemeanor. You will be instantly arrested. The punishment for the offense can be as much as a $2,000 fine and up to six months in jail.

4. Violation of License Restriction: one example of a violation of a driver's license restriction is if you must wear corrective lenses while driving and you get caught without them, in addition to a ticket with a fine of up to $200, your license may be suspended.

5. Unlawful or Fraudulent use of a License: This means lending your license to someone or altering it in any way. More about altering licenses will be discussed below. This is an automatic suspension of one year for the first offense.

6. "Driving Under the Influence" (DUI) or "Minor in Possession of Alcohol" (MIP): Anyone under the age of twenty-one with any detectible amount of alcohol can be ticketed, or arrested, if driving. If you are a minor and in possession of alcohol without a parent present, you may be ticketed. Along with having to complete sanctions, your license, or your ability to get one, will be suspended for thirty days. You must also attend a Texas-approved Alcohol-Awareness Course or your driving privileges will be suspended for up to a year.

7. Driving While Intoxicated (DWI): This suspension is for not less than ninety days or more than 365 days for a first offense. The penalty increases for subsequent DWIs.

8. Refusal to take the breath test: Your license will be confiscated, taken by the arresting officer at the time of arrest, and suspended immediately. You will have only fifteen days to request a hearing to get it back. Even if the DWI charge is dismissed, the suspension is not less than ninety days if you are twenty-one or older. If you are under twenty-one, the suspension is for one year. Realize, if you refuse a request for a breath test, the officer will generally request a warrant from a magistrate for your blood (see § 4.67 for more information).

   Special Note: More and more, officers are simply requesting a blood test if a person is going to be charged with DWI. If you refuse, the officer will request a warrant that you must give your blood from a magistrate.

9. Scoring .08 or higher on the breath test: If you are arrested for DWI and score a .08 or higher on the breath test, your license is automatically suspended for not less than sixty days, whether or not you are prosecuted for DWI.

10. Being at fault in an accident for damages and failing to pay: If you are at fault in an accident, and there is any personal injury or property damage of $1,000 or more, and you fail to pay the damages, your license may be suspended UNTIL YOU PAY. The license may be reinstated two years from the date of the accident, if no lawsuit has been filed against you. If a lawsuit is filed and you lose, regardless of the amount of damages, the suspension lasts UNTIL YOU PAY.

11. Failure to Maintain Financial Responsibility (FMFR), which means "no insurance": upon a *second conviction* of "Failure to Maintain Financial Responsibility" (FMFR), your license may be suspended UNTIL YOU GET INSUR-ANCE, unless you immediately obtain such insurance and provide proof to the court. (Doesn't happen very often but the sheriff may also confiscate your vehicle until proof of insurance is provided . . . something to know.)

12. Ignoring an out-of-state ticket: If you receive an out-of-state ticket and ignore it, the odds are that you will receive a notice from the DPS. This notice tells you your license will be suspended unless you take care of the ticket.

13. Felony drug conviction: this suspension is for 180 days.

14. Being under twenty-one and convicted of DWI or drug offenses: Your license is suspended for twelve months on a first offense. This runs concurrently (at the same time) with a suspension for test refusal.

In most of the above-listed situations, you are entitled to a hearing before your license is revoked. Notice for this is mailed to the address on your license. You may be granted probation if you are a first-time offender. There is no probation if you are suspended under number 10 above. Most of the time there is no probation under numbers 8 or 9 either.

True Story

Steven Anyone is twenty-one years old. His brother, Trey, is not. Steven agrees to trade driver's licenses for the weekend. (I'll leave it to your imagination as to why Trey might want to appear to be twenty-one.)

Steven is driving his car, upon which he has just placed oversized tires. The speedometer reads 40 mph, which is the speed limit. Therefore, Steven is very surprised to be stopped by the police.

The officer asks for Steven's license. Panic City! Steven only has Trey's license. Either he shows no license at all, in which case he'll get a ticket for Failure to Display a Driver's License, or he gives the officer Trey's license.

Once again, Steven makes the wrong choice. He gives the officer Trey's license, hoping for only a warning.

The officer says to Steven, "Where are your glasses?" Steven had forgotten that Trey has to wear glasses to drive.

Steven replies, "I left them at home." The officer then says that he stopped Steven for speeding. Steven (pretending to be Trey) says that his speedometer read 40 mph. The officer then tells Steven that oversized tires make the speedometer inaccurate, unless you alter the speedometer.

The officer then tickets Steven, in Trey's name, for Speeding and a driver's license restriction of not wearing glasses when required.

Poor Steven. He has now entangled himself in a costly mess and has dragged Trey into it, too.

If they keep quiet about the deception, Trey will have traffic convictions on his record.

If they tell the truth, Steven will get a ticket for Speeding and another one for presenting a license not his own. Trey will get a ticket for allowing his license to be used by someone else. They then both may face license suspension.

Steven could have avoided all of this by refusing to lend his license. There is always the potential Trey might get caught using it too, and then they'd both face license suspension for sure.

Even if Steven did trade licenses, he could have avoided most of the trouble by telling the officer that he didn't have his license with him (perfectly true). He would then have been ticketed for Speeding and Failure to Display. The Failure to Display charge would be dismissed by the court when Steven showed his valid license. Nobody would have faced suspension, as long as Trey didn't get caught!

2.15. Fake or Altered Licenses

If you alter your own license, have it altered, purchase or use a false license, give false information to obtain a license, or lend your license to someone else, you face numerous penalties, as listed below. The penalties are even more serious if you make false licenses.

1. Lending your license or possessing more than one license: Class C misdemeanor, punishable by a fine up to $500. (*Note*: Your license is also subject to suspension.)
2. False swearing on an application: usually a Class C misdemeanor, punishable by a fine up to $500.
3. Use of a license with false information on it: Class A misdemeanor, punishable by up to one year in jail and a fine up to $3,000.
4. Possession, use, or manufacture of a document deceptively similar to a driver's license: Class C misdemeanor, punishable by a fine up to $500.
5. Counterfeit or forged license (note that this is different from item [4] above)—either the making, sale, or possession of a counterfeit or forged license—FELONY: two to five years in the state penitentiary under the traffic code or, under the penal code, a third-degree felony, punishable by two to twenty years and/or a fine not to exceed $10,000.

Remember that your license can be suspended for one year under all of the above offenses.

Because the legal drinking age is twenty-one, many young people are tempted to do some or all of the offenses listed above. Be aware of the risks you run.

Driver Responsibility Program (DRP)

Special Note: The whole DRP is being discussed in the current 85th legislative session. This program may be substantially altered or even repealed. As of the time of this writing, the following is how it stands.

2.16. Surcharges!

Found in chapter 708 of the Texas Transportation Code, the DRP requires the Department of Public Safety to apply surcharges to certain traffic convictions. This surcharge or administrative fee, as it is called, is charged to a driver based on the number of *points* or *convictions*. Points are assigned to your driving record with every moving traffic conviction even if you don't have a driver's license.

2.17. Point System

Points are applied for moving traffic violation convictions and remain on the driver's record for *three years*. Points are assigned as follows:

- Texas moving violation = two points
- Out-of-state moving violation = two points
- Texas moving violation resulting in a crash = three points
- Out-of-state moving violation resulting in a crash = three points

If you get six or more points within a three-year period, surcharges will be assessed by the State of Texas. You will be required to pay a one-hundred-dollar surcharge for the first six points and an additional twenty-five dollars for every point after six. The surcharge will be assessed every year you maintain six points or more. DPS will review your points every year, so your points and surcharges may vary.

2.18. Convictions

Drivers who are convicted of one or more of the offenses listed below will pay a yearly surcharge (that's every year) for *three years* from the date of each conviction. No points are applied for these offenses since the surcharge is automatic upon conviction.

- Driving without a license—no driver's license, no commercial driver's license, expired license, or endorsement violation—up to $100
- Driving While License Invalid (DWLI)—driver's license is canceled, suspended, denied renewal, or revoked—$250
- Failure to Maintain Financial Responsibility or FMFR (no insurance)—up to $250
- Intoxication—first offense, Texas or out-of-state conviction for driving (DWI), intoxication assault, or manslaughter—$1,000
- Intoxication—second, third, or more offenses, Texas or out-of-state conviction for driving (DWI), intoxication assault, or manslaughter—$1,500
- DWI with blood-alcohol concentration of 0.16 (twice the legal limit) or greater—Texas or out-of-state conviction—$2,000

Real Life Example: Say you are driving and you have never had a driver's license. Because you don't have a DL you know you are driving illegally. We all know illegal drivers cannot be covered by insurance, so if you are pulled over, you could be written tickets for both charges. No DL and FMFR. If convicted in court, not only would you pay the court the fine and court costs, but surcharges will also be assessed. DPS will assess a surcharge up to one hundred dollars for the No-DL conviction. For the no-insurance conviction, a surcharge up to $250 will be assessed. That is up to $350. You could have taken a driver's education class for $350 and had money left over. Now here is where it gets really bad for you. Like mentioned above those surcharges are assessed for three years, $350 a year for three years. Yep, $1,050, because you "didn't have time to take a driver's ed. course."

2.19. How Will You Be Notified If You Receive a Surcharge?

You will receive notice through the mail to the address listed on your Texas driver's license or Texas ID. Remember, you are legally required to change the address on your license or ID within thirty days of moving. Your surcharge must be paid within 105 days to prevent suspension of your driving privileges.

If you would like to change the address on your license or ID online, visit www.dps.texas.gov/DriverLicense, and look under "Online Services."

2.20. Do You Have to Pay the Full Amount of the Surcharge at One Time?

You may pay the surcharge in installments (payment plan) but will be charged a $2.50 service fee for each payment. Failing to make a monthly payment will result in suspension of your driving privileges. On the payment plan, you may only get your license back by keeping up the minimum monthly payment or by paying the balance in full.

2.21. Sometimes DRP will Send Notice for Only Four or Five Points

This is an "advisory" notice and is informational only. This notice will let you know that any additional traffic convictions will result in a point surcharge. No payment is due at this point. But ANY MORE and surcharges are right around the corner. START DRIVING BETTER!

2.22. What Happens If You Don't Pay?

You will be suspended, and if pulled over by an officer, may be charged with "Driving While License Invalid." The first conviction for this charge is a Class C misdemeanor with a fine of up to $500. After the first conviction, the next one is a Class B misdemeanor with a punishment of up to $2,000 and/or up to six months in jail.

2.23. How Do You Pay?

Get to thinking, because you only have 104 days to decide. Day 105 it is due. You may pay the first year's surcharge or, if you have the money, pay all three years up front. If this is not an option, you may set up a payment plan with the state. Whatever you choose, remember only 105 days.

Your license can also be suspended for medical reasons, Failure to Stop and Render Aid in an accident, and Vehicular Homicide.

For more information on points or surcharges go to www.txsurchargeonline.com

2.24 Texas Department of Public Safety Omni Program

There is also a service used by courts for defendants that simply don't pay. It is called Omni. If you decide you aren't going to pay for any citation (ticket), the court with jurisdiction will place an Omni hold on your driver's license. This hold will keep you from renewing your driver's license when it is time. A 30 percent surcharge is added to the total of your ticket and must be paid before the hold is lifted.

For more information on Omni holds or to see if you have one, go to www.texasfailuretoappear.com, and click on "Search" at the top of the page.

Tickets and Insurance

2.25. Effects of Convictions on Your Insurance

The effect a ticket has on your insurance depends on the type of insurance policy you have and your insurance company. If you can't find on your policy the name of any of the types listed below, ask your insurance agent. A ticket taken care of by a Driving Safety Course (DSC) or Deferred Disposition can't be used against you.

Generally speaking, if you have:

1. State Set Rate Plan (with deviations up or down): Individual tickets as they occur do not automatically increase the premium. However, if you get enough convictions in a policy period (three is a common number), your company may refuse to renew your policy at the same rate. Accidents can increase the premium.
2. Texas Insurance Plan (high or assigned risk): When you have a bad driving record, are under age twenty-five, or have no previous driving history in the United States, this may be the only kind of policy you can get. It is expensive, and each ticket increases the expense.

Special Note: If you are on a policy with your family, then the insurance company counts the entire family's tickets together for purposes of cancellation or premium increases.

If you are legally entitled to possess a driver's license, you are entitled to insurance coverage, but it may not be with the company you want or at the price you want to pay.

Vehicular Insurance

This section is intended as a basic look at insurance for cars and motorcycles. For specifics, you should read your insurance policy contract. Many contracts are written in plain English. For further information, contact your insurance agent or the State Board of Insurance. For information on making a claim on your insurance, see the sections on traffic accidents (§ 3.32 and following).

2.26. How to Find Insurance

Shop online or in the yellow pages of your telephone directory. You will find insurance companies and insurance agents listed.

The insurance agents sell the policy to you. They do not process the claims or make the rules. They are either independent agents who represent several different companies or tied agents who only represent a single company.

Shop around for the best price. Be sure that you give accurate information on your driving record, age, and the year, model, and make of your car. All of that information is used to fix the cost of your policy.

The State Board of Insurance sets the maximum rate, but some companies offer coverage for less.

2.27. What State Law Requires

The State of Texas requires that you have your vehicle covered by a liability policy with coverage amounts of $20,000/$40,000/$15,000, commonly referred to as the 20/40/15 limit. This is the least amount of insurance you can carry.

What does 20/40/15 mean? The first two figures, 20/40, mean the total amount that will be paid to a single person for injuries in that accident is $20,000, and that in any accident the total amount of insurance coverage available to be paid for personal injuries is $40,000. If you have this minimum coverage, the following examples will help you understand how it works:

1. Only one person is injured, and the bills add up to $30,000.
   Your policy will pay only $20,000 to one person, even
   though your total policy limit for one accident is $40,000.
   YOU ARE PERSONALLY RESPONSIBLE FOR THE REMAIN-
   ING $10,000.
2. Three people are injured, and the total bill is $60,000.
   Your policy will pay only $40,000 divided among the three
   injured people and no more than $20,000 to any one person.
   YOU ARE RESPONSIBLE FOR THE REMAINING $20,000.

In our 20/40/15 policy, the figure 15 refers to property damage. This usually means the other vehicle but also means the light pole or fence or house that you struck. The policy will pay a maximum of $15,000 for property damage. Any amount over that must come from you.

Because potential medical bills can be so expensive and because car repair and value is so high, MOST COMPANIES RECOMMEND THAT YOU CARRY COVERAGE WITH HIGHER LIMITS to protect yourself.

2.28. Premium

A premium is the price YOU pay to obtain an insurance policy; in other words, it's the actual cost to you and what you pay. You will usually pay your premiums monthly or, if a baller, up to six months or a year in advance.

2.29. Deductible

Most types of insurance coverage have a "deductible." This means you pay the damage yourself until the deductible amount is reached. The insurance company pays the rest. If your deductible is $250, then you pay the first $250 of any accident. The higher the deductible, the lower the policy premium (monthly price). A liability policy has no deductible. There are always deductibles on uninsured motorist, collision, fire, theft, and vandalism coverage.

Types of Coverage

2.30. Liability

To comply with state law, as mentioned above you must have at least this coverage. This type of policy means that *if you are at fault* in a crash, and the other party is injured or has property damage, your insurance will pay for the other party's actual damage and/or injuries up to the limits of your policy (remember 20/40/15). Liability DOES NOT pay for your own injuries or damage to your vehicle. Liability will pay for injuries to your passenger if your passenger sues you.

Again, this is the bare minimum required by law. Even if you are trying to pay the least you can for insurance, it would be wise to add a few things to liability. The cost for some of these extra coverages is very small. Some of those extras are listed below.

2.31. Uninsured Motorist Coverage

Lots and lots and lots of people are still driving around without insurance, even though we all know it is against the law. If an uninsured motorist is at fault in a crash with you and you only have liability coverage, you have a problem. Technically, the uninsured motorist should pay for your damages out of his or her own pocket, but think about it. Many uninsured motorists have nothing. You may be left to repair your own damage, while you try to collect from the uninsured motorist.

If you have uninsured motorist insurance coverage, your problem is solved. You pay the deductible ($250 is common), and your insurance coverage pays the rest. Then the insurance company tries to collect from the uninsured motorist. This coverage is valuable and typically adds little to the cost of the policy. The Texas legislature thinks so highly of it that they passed a law requiring you to sign a paper saying you don't want this coverage, if you get only liability coverage.

2.32. Underinsured Motorist Coverage

Sometimes linked with uninsured motorist coverage, this coverage takes care of you in a different circumstance. If the motorist who hit you has insurance but has only the minimum 20/40/15 policy, and YOUR injuries total $30,000, then his or her insurance will pay you only $20,000, the policy limit. The underinsured motorist himself or herself owes you the remaining $10,000. Could you come up with the money to pay someone $10,000? Probably he or she can't either. If you have underinsured motorist coverage, you claim on it for the additional $10,000. Your insurance company will then seek to recover from the underinsured motorist who hit you. Adding this coverage to your policy will cost very little.

2.33. Personal Injury Protection (PIP)

This optional coverage will pay for personal injury to you or your passengers, when you are at fault in a crash. It is available in such specific amounts of coverage as $2,500, $5,000, or $10,000 per accident. This is the only type of vehicle insurance coverage that covers your own injuries, if you are at fault. Your own medical insurance will cover you in most accidents, so you may elect not to add this coverage, even though it is very cheap.

Special Note: You may want to have this coverage for your passengers. Your own medical policy will not cover them, unless they are family members covered by your medical insurance policy. If they are not, there is no personal injury coverage on your car insurance, UNLESS they sue you in court. In that case, your liability coverage pays. The liability coverage only pays if there is a lawsuit. Without PIP, you force your friends to sue you to be covered by your insurance.

2.34. Collision

This is also optional, *unless you are still paying for your car*. If you are, the terms of your loan agreement REQUIRE that you have this coverage. Collision coverage pays to repair your car when you are at fault in an accident. There is a deductible ($250 is common).

2.35. Fire, Theft, and Vandalism

This is just what it says. If your car is damaged in one of those ways or by a natural disaster (like a tornado), this coverage pays. There is a deductible, usually smaller than the other deductibles ($100 is common).

2.36. What Kind of Coverage Is Right for You?

If you are still paying on the car, you must carry all of the above, except for PIP. If your car is paid for, you are only required to carry liability (remember the 20/40/15 scenario?). I suggest you find out the cost of the various additional coverages and then decide. Remember, if you have only liability coverage and your car is damaged, stolen, or never recovered, you are out the money.

2.37. What Is Not Covered?

Read the policy. It lists specific exclusions. Unlicensed drivers are not covered. PEOPLE WITH NO LICENSE SHOULD NOT DRIVE. People with a learner's permit are covered only if they are driving legally with a licensed driver is in the front seat. Automobile policies do not cover motorcycles, off-road vehicles, and so forth. A basic policy does not cover you if you use your car in your business all the time. It does cover you driving to and from work though. If you use your car in business more than this—if you deliver pizza or drive for UBER, for example—you must tell the insurance company, and they will draw up a policy to cover you. You are not covered if you rent your car to someone else. You are not covered in the event of war or riot. YOU ARE NOT COVERED IF YOU DRIVE INTO MEXICO.

2.38. Unexpected Coverage

Your policy does cover you if you drive someone else's car. Your policy also covers you if you lend (not rent) your car to a legally licensed driver. Your policy covers you if you rent a car.

Types of Plans

As I mentioned earlier in the section on the effects of traffic tickets on insurance costs, two insurance plans are common in Texas. Your record, or for a family policy, the entire family's record, determines the plan for which you qualify.

Tickets that you take care of by attending a Driving Safety Course (DSC) CANNOT be used to increase insurance rates under either plan. Even if you don't have a ticket, some insurance companies will give you a discount if you take a Driving Safety Course. Some insurance companies will even give a discount if you keep your grades at a certain level. It is always smart to shop around and see what is offered.

2.39. State Set Rate Plan with Deviations

Most drivers over age twenty-five have this type of plan. The base rate (premium) is set by the state. Companies consider what type of risk you are and then give you a discount on the state rate (deviation downward) or add to the state base rate (deviation upward). If you are over twenty-five and have no tickets on your record for the last three years, you may get a deviation on your premium for as much as 25 percent less than the state rate. If you have a child who becomes a driver at age sixteen, even though that sixteen-year-old has no tickets, you will lose that 25 percent downward deviation and probably receive an upward deviation above the state rate. Drivers aged sixteen to twenty-five statistically have a higher risk of accidents, so your insurance will cost more. Sorry.

Individual tickets cannot cause your premium to increase. However, if you or your family receive enough tickets within a short time period, your insurance company may refuse to renew your policy at the same rate. There will be an upward deviation in the new premium. "Enough" tickets may be as few as three in twelve months. The company determines how many are "enough." Remember, it doesn't mean three tickets per person but a three-ticket total for all of those in your family covered under the plan.

You are also penalized for accidents and Driving While Intoxicated (DWI) convictions.

2.40. Texas Insurance Plan (High or Assigned Risk)

The state does NOT set rates on this type of policy. If you have a bad driving record, have no previous driving history in the United States, or are considered a bad risk for any other reason, this may be the only type of insurance you can buy. The premium can be 75 to 200 percent higher than the state set rate. Shop around. The rates will vary greatly from company to company.

Each ticket, accident, or DWI conviction increases the policy premium (your cost).

Just remember. If you keep a good driving record when you reach age twenty-six, your insurance rates will drop a lot.

2.41. State Board of Insurance

Any complaints about insurance agents or companies can be made in writing to:

Texas State Board of Insurance
Claims and Complaints
P.O. Box 149104
Austin, Texas 78714-9104
(1-800) 252-3439
http://www.tdi.texas.gov/

Chapter 3

DRIVING WHILE YOUNG

Traffic Tickets

In case you've been so lucky as to have reached this age without being pulled over by the police or receiving a ticket, I'll begin with the basics. Remember, the more you know, the less threatened you may feel.

3.1. When You See the Red and Blue Lights, Pull Over!

Even if you don't think the officer means you, pull over. Few things make an officer madder than to have someone delay stopping. Usually the siren or loudspeaker is used only as a last resort. Don't wait. Find the safest place, but pull over and pull over now. If the officer doesn't want you, he or she will go on past and no harm is done. If the officer does mean you, then we need to start with some commonsense advice on your role in that encounter. Some of the officer's procedures may appear unnecessary, but keep in mind even the most routine traffic stop can be potentially dangerous. By understanding what is going to happen and what will be expected of you ahead of time, we may eliminate some possible misunderstandings. Keep in mind law enforcement is both difficult and dangerous. Officers must constantly be aware of not only the safety of those they are sworn to protect but also their own safety too.

You should pull over to the right side of the roadway and stop your car as far out of the lane of traffic as possible. Go ahead and turn your radio off, and roll down your driver's window. If your back windows are tinted, it is smart to roll them down too. If it is dark outside, turning on your interior and hazard lights will make everyone more comfortable. Stay calm, and, if you have passengers, ask them to stay quiet and calm too. Stay seated and in the car unless you are asked to step out. As the officer approaches, put those hands at ten and two o'clock, that is, on the steering wheel and in plain sight. Keep in mind the officer is watching carefully for weapons and to make sure nothing is being hidden.

Special Note: To those of you who grew up watching certain TV shows and movies in which the civilian always outruns the officer—getting pulled over is REALITY, not TV. In real life, the officers are better drivers, there are more of them, they have radios, and they always get you in the end.

True Story

A motorcycle can always outrun a car, right? Not necessarily.

Steven Anyone is riding his brand-new motorcycle on the city streets for the first time. He is so carried away with enjoyment that he neglects to make a complete stop at a stop sign. His enjoyment turns to horror when he glances back and sees a police car right behind him with the red and blue lights on.

Panic City strikes again! His motorcycle is unregistered, uninspected, and uninsured, and he has a license but is unlicensed for a motorcycle. Without thinking, he accelerates, and the chase is on.

Several blocks and numerous traffic violations later, Steven is headed for an intersection with a very busy street. Ignoring the stop sign would be suicidal. He attempts a quick stop. Alas, the intersection was newly graveled. The wheels skid as the motorcycle keeps sliding toward the busy street. Self-preservation gives him only one option. He lays the bike down on the street.

Steven ends up with a wrecked motorcycle, assorted cuts and bruises, and NINE TICKETS. Each ticket carries a fine of up to $200, not to mention what those tickets will do to his insurance.

Steven ends up a sadder, poorer, but a wiser man. (His lawyer ends up richer.)

3.2. Seat Belts

The law requires that the driver and all passengers wear seat belts and shoulder harnesses. After you've stopped, DON'T RELEASE YOUR SEAT BELT UNTIL the officer has approached your window and seen it or orders you out of the car. If you release it as soon as you stop, you may be ticketed for NO SEAT BELT, because the officer did not see you wearing it. This ticket carries a fine of not less than twenty-five or more than fifty dollars, but with court costs added will be about $150.

3.3. Identification

Be prepared to present your valid driver's license and current insurance. Although most officers will tell you why you were pulled over, you do not have to be told before you comply. If you have to reach for your license, tell the officer where you are reaching. Express your movements. For example, "my insurance is in the glove box; I need to get it." Move slowly. Put your hands back on the steering wheel while the officer checks your license and insurance. If you have a valid license but don't have it with you, DON'T PANIC. A ticket for "Failure to Display a Driver's License" will be dismissed when you show the license to the appropriate court. If you have an expired license or never had a driver's license, the fine is any amount up to $200. Possession of an altered license or false license can mean big trouble (see § 2.15 for further information).

Special Note: Almost all automobile insurance policies REQUIRE that you have a current, valid license for the policy to be effective. If you have let your license expire, your insurance may not be in effect until you renew the license. A lost or stolen license can be replaced upon payment of a small fee. Suspended licenses are discussed elsewhere (§ 2.14).

You have the right and should always ask for identification especially if the officer is not in uniform or if the patrol unit is unmarked as a police squad car. If the officer is in uniform, his or her name and badge number will be at the bottom of any documentation he or she gives you. Most police agencies have a procedure that they must keep records of every traffic stop. Some require the officer to complete a warning if a citation (ticket) is not issued. This procedure keeps track of the officer's activity as well as documenting for you the officer's reasoning for the stop. The officer will turn the same documentation in to his or her department and the court with jurisdiction.

3.4. Proof of Insurance

As discussed in chapter 2, all drivers (Texas residents and nonresidents alike) must carry proof of liability insurance. What you may be unaware of is that you must present that proof upon demand. If you are stopped by the police, it will be demanded. In Texas, most insurance companies provide a billfold-size proof of policy card complete with effective times and dates. It is also acceptable to present a digital version on your smart phone. If you don't have proof with you, you will be ticketed. The legal term for this charge is "Failure to Maintain Financial Responsibility" (FMFR). If you later prove that you had a policy in effect at the time of the ticket, the court will dismiss this ticket with no fines or fees. The punishment, if you had no insurance in effect, is as follows:

First offense: $175–$350 fine, plus court costs
Second offense: $350–$500 fine, plus court costs

In addition, your vehicle may be impounded until you obtain insurance. You will be required to keep it in effect for two years or have your license and car registration suspended.

Special Note: Your verification (proof) of insurance has the time and date of your policy. That is, if you get a citation at noon, and then at 1 p.m. go buy insurance, it doesn't cover the earlier citation. It's good that you now have insurance as you are required, but think about something. If you cause a crash at noon, then a 1:00 p.m. go and buy insurance, will the insurance company cover your accident? Nope! Sorry, doesn't work for tickets either.

For more about specific types of insurance, see § 2.25.

3.5. Warrant Check

The police officer will check your name, date of birth, and license number for any outstanding warrants via computer. Don't be surprised if other patrol units arrive. Remember, chances are great that your interaction is being recorded both with video and sound. This is done for everyone's safety. Answer questions politely and honestly, but be brief. Remain calm and respectful. If you are seventeen years old or older and any warrants do appear, most probably you will be arrested. You must then either pay the fine or post a bond (more about bonds in § 4.4) to be released on the warrant AND maybe on any new ticket the officer may have just issued to you. Any tickets issued by a Texas highway patrolman that are overdue and unpaid or overdue tickets from the city police of the city or county in which you are being stopped will be listed in that computer check as well.

3.6. Don't Argue with the Officer

This is a big one! If the officer asks for an explanation, give it in a calm voice and a respectful manner. However mad you may be at the officer, it is STUPID to argue or be disrespectful. This is not a personal attack. The officer has a job to do. Most officers will be courteous, but even if the officer is not courteous, stay cool, calm, and polite. Remember, like it or not, the officer is in charge of the situation. The use of profane, vulgar, or obscene language or gestures in a public place is a violation of the disorderly conduct law. YOU CAN BE ARRESTED for breaking it. The momentary pleasure you get from cursing or gesturing is not worth a night in jail and a fine of up to $500 (more about Disorderly Conduct in § 4.17). Typically, the officer wants to do his or her job and send you down the road. If you are issued a ticket, stay polite and DO NOT ARGUE. The side of the roadway is not a place to play lawyer. It never works out. The best place to show a police officer that he or she is wrong is not at the time of the traffic stop, it's later in court.

Special Note: Your best option is to COMPLY NOW AND COMPLAIN LATER. If the officer is attempting to do something illegal or immoral, then, even under those circumstances, there probably are better ways of remedying that than in getting into a conflict with the officer on the side of the road. When you are told to do something by a police officer, the best and safest course of action is to do it. If you feel as if your constitutional rights have been violated or you are being mistreated, you will have a chance later to complain to the appropriate authorities. (For information about making a complaint, see chapter 8.)

3.7. Sign the Ticket

Signing the ticket in Texas is NEVER admitting you are guilty. It is only your promise that you will contact the court. The ticket uses the legal term "appear"—within the specified time limit (usually about ten days). If you refuse to sign the ticket, you are refusing to contact the court on your own. The officer has no choice but to arrest you.

3.8. Mistakes on the Ticket

Mistakes on the ticket DO NOT usually result in a ticket being dismissed. A misspelled name, the wrong date, time, sex, license number, vehicle description, or location DOES NOT get a ticket dismissed. The only way to use these errors to your advantage is to go to trial. At that trial, when cross-examining the officer, you can point out the errors for the judge or jury. You may point out that if the officer made mistakes on the ticket, maybe he or she was mistaken about the offense, too.

3.9. Showing the Speed Locked-In on Radar

The officer DOES NOT have to show you the speed you are accused of going "locked-in" on radar. No matter where this old rumor started, let it end here.

3.10. Tickets for Expired Registration

Courts will dismiss a ticket for Expired Registration for a twenty-dollar fee upon proof of your renewal. This charge can only be dismissed if the registration was expired for sixty days or less (more about registration in § 8.39).

3.11. Which Law Enforcement Agency Gave You the Ticket?

If you lose your ticket, knowing which agency issued it to you will simplify things. The Texas Highway Patrol (also known as the Department of Public Safety or DPS) can issue a ticket to you anywhere. As their name implies, they most often give tickets on the highway or interstate. Normally, a DPS ticket goes to the justice of the peace court to be processed. City and town police give tickets in a variety of sizes and colors. They normally only ticket inside the city and town limits, but they can follow, or chase, you outside the city. Don't think you can escape them by leaving their city or town limits. Municipal courts usually handle police tickets. County sheriff's deputies do less traffic enforcement than the DPS or city police. Deputies have the authority to do traffic enforcement, if they so choose. Their tickets also vary in size and color and normally go to the justice of the peace court.

3.12. Time Limit on the Ticket

By law, the time limit must be at least ten days. Some courts allow you more time. READ THE TICKET. This is where it gets a little *sticky* for you as the reader. The law changes for you on your seventeenth birthday. If you are sixteen years old or younger at the time you are charged with a violation you must appear in open court with a parent or guardian. Most courts will notify you and your parent or guardian of a court date by mail addressed to the address listed on your citation (ticket). Your parent, guardian, or conservator must appear with you, or he or she may be charged with a Class C misdemeanor. The court must allow you at least ten days before you are due in court. At this initial court hearing, the judge will explain your rights and all of your options. He or she will answer any questions you may have. Expect to enter a plea at this hearing (see § 3.14).

One other thing: if you do have contact with a police officer and are charged with an offense, make sure to tell your parent or guardian. There is nothing worse than coming home from a great day and seeing mom standing there with a summons from the court.

If you are seventeen or older, you can usually take care of most court appearances at the court clerk's window, by mail and, with more and more courts, by email. Although the ticket uses the words appear *before the court*, this is a legal term. It does not necessarily mean that you must *appear* in person. Whatever way you choose to do it, make sure you CONTACT THE COURT. If you need more than ten days to come up with the money, most courts will work with you to give you extra time, within reason, if you contact the court before the ten days are up.

3.13. Informally Handling the Ticket

Many people say they just want "to talk to the judge," not have a real trial. Some judges will allow this. Most will not. Justices of the peace are more likely to allow it, but not all of them will. This "informal talk" can never be done before you enter a plea (see § 3.14) and seldom results in a ticket dismissal. It is unreasonable to expect the judge to dismiss a ticket based only on your story. It is only fair that he or she hears what the officer has to say, too. That is what a trial is for. Remember, the law is the law no matter what offense you are charged with. Can you imagine a judge allowing a murderer to come into the office and discuss his or her case? It's not going to happen. Some people want this "informal talk" to admit they are guilty but had a "good reason" for speeding or running that stop sign. The most you can reasonably expect a judge to do in those circumstances is reduce the fine. Ask for the "informal talk" if you want to, but don't be surprised if it is not granted or does not turn out the way you had hoped.

Going to Court

3.14. Entering a Plea

You may make any one of three pleas:

1. Guilty: A Guilty plea is an admission of guilt. No "ifs," "ands," or "buts," "I did it." It requires you to pay the fine, perform community service, attend a Driving Safety Course (DSC), or request a Deferred Disposition. (See "Alternative Sentencing" for DSC and Deferred Disposition in § 3.19.)
2. No Contest: Also known by the Latin phrase *Nolo Contendere*. You automatically enter this plea if you just pay the ticket. This plea DOES NOT admit guilt but says that you don't want to have a trial (contest) on the matter. You will be responsible for the fine with this plea too. You may also request community service, DSC, or a Deferred Disposition.
3. Not Guilty: You enter this plea if you want to have a trial on the issue. In most courts, you will be required to post a bond to guarantee that you'll show up at the trial (see more about appearance bonds in § 4.4).

After a Not Guilty plea, the next step is usually a pre-trial hearing. You will return to the court on a specific date and have the opportunity to speak individually with the prosecutor. Pre-trial is the time to make any motions you may have or see any evidence that the state (the prosecutor is considered "the state" in all court hearings) has against you. Be prepared, and ask any and all questions you may have. Tell your story if you want. Share your thoughts on why you feel you are not guilty of the offense charged, but remember the prosecutor's job is to see that justice is done. If you and the prosecutor cannot come to some conclusion, your case will be set for trial. The trial will be held in the county or town where you got the ticket. You have the option to have a trial before the judge alone or before a jury. The trial will normally be at some time in the future weeks or months.

3.15. Failure to Appear (FTA)

If you fail to contact the court ("appear") within the time limit, the judge can issue a second charge, called a "Failure to Appear" or a "Violate Promise to Appear." Normally you will be notified of this by mail sent to the address on your original ticket. This FTA charge carries a fine usually over $200 by itself. The amount is up to the judge. Generally speaking, there is no legally acceptable reason for failing to appear, so GET TO THE COURT ON TIME. "I forgot" or "I lost the ticket" cuts no ice with most judges.

3.16. Warrant for Your Arrest

If you ignore the "Failure to Appear," and you are at least seventeen years old, the judge may issue a warrant for your arrest. This can be served on you by an officer coming to arrest you if you're nearby. If you are not, the court may enter it in the statewide computer and wait for you to be stopped for something else.

Special Note: Most judges simply want you to take care of your responsibility. If you sign a citation and promise to appear, they expect you to do just that. If you really did forget and make it to the court on your own, without contact with a police officer, the court will usually work with you to take care of your business, but don't expect that extra charge of "Failure to Appear" to just go away.

3.17. Options with the Court

On Class C misdemeanors (tickets), you generally have the following three options. We will discuss each with a more in-depth explanation below:

1. Take care of the fine (requires a plea of Guilty or No Contest),
2. Request alternative sentencing: Driving Safety Course (DSC) or Deferred Disposition (requires a plea of Guilty or No Contest),
3. Or go to trial (requires a plea of Not Guilty).

Special Note: Typically, you will see and spend most of your time at the court with a court clerk. The clerk is a professional in the options you will have to dispose, or take care of, your case. Ask questions! You need to understand everything that will be expected of you by the court. Never sign something if you don't know exactly what you are signing. Be polite, and remember the clerk is not the reason you are there. He or she didn't break the law, didn't write you the citation, and doesn't set the fine. The clerk is not allowed to provide you legal advice. He or she is only there to help YOU dispose of YOUR case.

3.18. Taking Care of the Fine

With a few exceptions, such as the no-insurance ticket (remember, legally known as "Failure to Maintain Financial Responsibility" or FMFR), most traffic violations carry a fine of $0 to $200, plus court costs. Generally speaking, if you plead Guilty or No Contest, or are found Guilty at trial, you will be required to pay the fine set by the judge all at once. The exact amount is up to the judge, or if you go to a jury trial, the jury may decide. You may always request to pay these fines and costs in installments or by payment plan. Just ask. You also may request to work out the fine by performing community service. An application is usually required for both. Be honest on the application. Lying on an application for a payment plan or community service is a Class A misdemeanor with a fine of up to $4,000. Again, most courts are willing to work with you if they can see you are making a good faith effort to take care of your responsibility. Always ask what options you have.

3.19. Request Alternative Sentencing

Driving Safety Course (DSC): If you would like to keep the conviction from your violation, for most common traffic offenses, off your driving record, this is one of your options. You must possess a valid Texas driver's license and NOT have attended DSC in the last year. If these apply, you may request that you be allowed to attend DSC. Most judges require you to sign a sworn affidavit, stating you have not taken the course in the last twelve months and are not currently enrolled to take DSC for a different charge in another court. You will need to provide a copy of a valid driver's license, valid insurance, and your driving record. If the judge agrees, you will be required to pay only the court costs to the court. Usually about $114. Keep in mind the DSC itself will cost also. The amount will depend on where you go or how you take it. The course typically ranges from twenty-five to fifty dollars. If you complete the course within ninety days, the conviction DOES NOT go on your driving record for any purpose. A list of approved schools can be obtained from the court of the town where you intend to go to school, or you may look them up online. If you look them up online, make sure it is a school that is "Texas approved." The DSC will consist of two four-hour sessions if you complete it in person. Many restaurants offer a DSC and include a meal in the cost of the course. It is to your benefit to shop around. If you decide to complete the course online, you may take your time over several days.

Special Note 1: You must get court permission before you take the course. If you are seventeen years of age, usually you can do this over the phone, through the mail, by email, or always in person. Check the court website. Most have instructions and the request forms for DSC there. Certain courts—not many, but some—require that you appear in person to request DSC.

Special Note 2: DSC CANNOT be used to take care of a violation of reckless driving, no proof of insurance, passing a school bus, or driving more than twenty-five miles over the posted speed limit.

A Deferred Disposition (or deferral) is another alternative that you may request. This too must be requested when you enter a plea and, if completed, will result in NO conviction on your driving record for your violation. A "deferral" is a probationary period, with a court order stating that from one date to another you either will or will not do certain things. One example of something you won't do is get another ticket during the deferral period. The deferral period is up to 180 days and could contain provisions, such as going to counseling or attending tutorials, depending on your charge. A special expense fee is required (usually about the same price as the fine), and if you are under the age of twenty-five, you must take a Driving Safety Course too.

3.20. Go to Trial

Remember, municipal courts hear trials on tickets issued inside the city or town limits, usually written by city police officers. Justice of the peace courts hear trials on tickets issued outside the city limits but inside the county limits, usually written by the highway patrol (green ticket) or sheriff's deputies. The municipal court judge is either elected or appointed and is usually a lawyer in larger towns and cities. The justice court judge is the justice of the peace and is always elected. The justice of the peace is usually not a lawyer, except in some major metropolitan areas.

3.21. Appearance Bonds

In either court, if you ask for a trial, you will usually be required to post an appearance bond. This bond will be either cash or a "paper bond," which is a promise to pay money if you fail to appear for trial. When you appear for trial, the cash will be refunded (with no interest). If you fail to appear, the cash bond will be forfeited, and you will be found Guilty on the charge. The bond money becomes your fine. If a "paper bond" was used, a warrant for your arrest will be issued. As principal (that is, the one responsible), you—and the two sureties who cosigned the bond with you—must pay the amount of the bond to the court.

"Paper bonds" are somewhat difficult and sometimes costly to obtain for traffic violations. Most of the time, a "paper bond" is double the amount of the fine and costs. You can pay a professional bondsman a nonrefundable fee to post the paper bond on your behalf, or you can locate a blank "appearance-bond" form yourself online. You will need to find two people willing to cosign the bond with you. By signing, they are saying that they will pay to the court the cash amount of the bond if you don't show up for trial. The bond must be approved by the judge of the appropriate court. Overall, if you have it, the cash bond is usually much easier to do.

Judge or Jury?

Which kind of trial is right for you? If you hire a lawyer, let the lawyer choose. If you are representing yourself, there are many factors that you should consider. Here are a few to think about. Keep in mind if you decide to represent yourself in a trial you will still be expected to know court procedure. Now is the time to show how mature you can be. Look at the advantages and disadvantages. Weigh those pros and cons.

3.22. Bench Trial/If a Judge Decides

ADVANTAGES:
1. Trial date is usually set quicker.
2. Usually the judge will not increase the amount of the fine set before trial, if he or she finds you Guilty after the trial.
3. A person representing himself or herself may feel less intimidated before a judge than a six-person jury.

DISADVANTAGES:
1. In many jurisdictions, the judge may know the officer.
2. The judge may hold you more strictly to the letter of the law than a jury would.

3.23. Jury/Trial by Jury

ADVANTAGES:

1. Except in very small towns, the jury members seldom know you or the officers.
2. The jury may tend to put themselves in your place and not judge you so strictly by the letter of the law.
3. Six people must believe you are guilty rather than just one.

DISADVANTAGES:

1. In municipal court, juries assess guilt or innocence AND the fine unless you ask, before the trial begins, for the judge to assess the fine. If you elect for the jury to decide, they can only be told that the fine is from $0 to $200. They can't be told the judge's usual fine. You run the risk that the jury might set a higher fine than the judge would, if they find you Guilty.
2. The average age of a jury will usually be that of your parents or older. Older adults are sometimes more skeptical of the truthfulness of young adults than a judge might be.

3.24. Do You Need a Lawyer?

This is, after all, a real trial. An attorney will be there to represent the city or county. Although you are not entitled to a court-appointed attorney or lawyer on a Class C misdemeanor (ticket), you may be able to defend yourself adequately. If you feel as if you would be better served with a lawyer, check the cost by calling several. (See § 8.6 Finding and Hiring an Attorney.) If it is beyond your budget, do not panic. Usually, the judge will help you follow the correct procedure. Follow his or her instructions and stay polite.

3.25. Will the Officer Show Up?

Yes, most of the time. In Dallas or Houston, there is a greater chance that the officer won't show, and your case will then be dismissed.

3.26. Court Reporter

A court reporter records everything said in a trial. This reporter is available in some municipal courts and is optional. A recording of the trial is useful in some types of appeal but generally not necessary for appeal to county court.

3.27. Which Option Is Right for You?

Should you pay the fine and costs, ask for alternative sentencing, or take it to trial? Well, it depends.

Factors to consider include the following:

1. How many tickets have you had before? If this is your very first ticket, paying it may be the cheapest way out but will you get the conviction and maybe points on your license? If this is your fourth ticket in twelve months and you pay it, you will probably lose your license, not to mention what it will do to your insurance rates (see notes on license suspension in § 2.14).
2. Where did you get the ticket? If you got the ticket 400 miles from home, it may not be realistic to return for a trial. If you got the ticket in your hometown, it may be a different story.
3. Are you eligible for a Driving Safety Course or a deferral? This is a good way to keep a conviction off your record.
4. How much is the fine?
5. What is the violation for? In some cases, there is no wiggle room. If you are accused of driving with only one headlight, you either were or you weren't. If you take this case to trial, the judge or jury is presented only with a one-fact issue. In this case, most people admit to driving with one headlight but want to give an explanation. No explanation can make you not guilty. (It might lessen the fine.) Keep in mind most courts consider this a "fix-it ticket." If you remedy the problem, i.e., fix the headlight, and show proof to the court, the charge against you may be dismissed.

6. How fast does the ticket allege you were going? The higher the speed, the harder it may be for a judge or jury to believe that it is a mistake.

7. What kind of vehicle do you drive? Fair or not, juries tend to disbelieve people who drive sports cars, souped-up cars, or motorcycles.

8. Are you already on Deferred Disposition (probation) for another ticket or for license suspension? Have you recently taken a Driving Safety Course for another violation?

If you are on DSC or Deferred Disposition already, one conviction during the term of probation will probably get your probation revoked.

Special Note: If you ask for a trial, you can change your mind and pay the fine or ask for DSC anytime until the beginning of the trial. If you go to trial and your case is called and you are found Guilty, the judge may allow you to attend DSC if you are eligible, BUT DON'T COUNT ON IT. It is up to the judge's discretion.

3.28. Some Basics If You Represent Yourself

For further information, see table 1.

1. Stay polite: Nobody likes a smart aleck. If you lose your temper, you will usually lose your case. Make your case more believable by showing mature behavior. If you are prepared and show that maturity, the judge will probably give you a little more leeway than if you act like a jerk.

2. Proper dress and appearance: The judge or jury will get their first impression of you from your appearance. Do the most to make that a good one. Dress as you would for church. Guys, that means at least a collared shirt, and no shorts. Everyone, leave the holey jeans and hard rock T-shirts at home. Subdue any unusual hairstyles. If your hair is purple, change it. You can always re-dye it after the trial. Rightly or wrongly, the more serious your demeanor

and dress, the more likely the judge or jury will believe you. Proclaiming your alternate style belongs in a different arena. Here, it will only hurt you.

3. Who goes first? The prosecution.

4. Selecting a jury: If you have selected to go to a trial by jury, STAY POLITE. You want a fair jury that doesn't know you or anyone else involved in the trial. If the main witness against you is an officer, ask if anyone is married to, related to, or close friends with the officer. Chances are high that person might tend to believe the officer rather than you. Be sure all potential jurors drive, especially on a traffic offense trial. You want only *drivers* on the jury, and maybe drivers who have had a ticket. You have the right to "strike" (mark through or remove) the names of three jurors on the jury list without giving a reason. The prosecution also has three strikes. The first six jurors not struck off the list will become the jury.

5. The trial begins: The trial will start with the prosecutor questioning the officer. DON'T INTERRUPT! Lawyers sometimes do with an objection, but you won't know what to object to, so stay quiet.

6. Cross-examination: You may ask the officer questions when the prosecutor is finished. STAY POLITE. Ask anything necessary to make the situation clearer. Be careful if you disagree with the officer's answer. Calling him or her a liar will NOT make points with the jury. You'll get your chance to talk later.

7. Your testimony: You cannot be made to testify if you don't want to, BUT in a traffic violation case, you may have no other way to tell your side of the story. If you do testify, tell your story as logically and briefly as you can. There will usually be a white-board that you can use, if necessary. If you contradict the officer, use words like "The officer must be mistaken," not "He [or she] is a liar."

8. The prosecutor's turn: If you do choose to testify the prosecutor will have the opportunity to cross-examine

you when you have finished with your testimony. STAY POLITE. Let him or her finish each question, and take a second (THINK) before you answer.

9. Other witnesses: If you have witnesses, they must appear in court in person. A written statement will not be allowed. You will question the witness first, and the prosecutor will cross-examine after.

10. The Verdict or Judgment: Either the jury retires to the jury room to reach a Verdict, or, if there is no jury, the judge decides. If the judge decides it is called a "Judgment."

Table 1. Outline of Procedure in a Criminal Trial

Step	Procedure
1	Select a jury (omit this step in a nonjury trial).
2	The chosen jury is impaneled and sworn in by the judge.
3	The trial begins. The judge will ask if you would like the "complaint" read to you. You have the right to receive a copy of the complaint twenty-four hours before the trial. All you have to do is ask. Once the complaint is read, or you waive the right to it being read, the judge will ask your plea one more time. If you plead "Not Guilty," the trial will proceed.
4	Opening argument by prosecution (optional).
5	Prosecution (State) calls and questions the first witness (usually the police officer on a traffic case).
6	Defendant (you) cross-examines (questions) the first witness. Questions only! Don't tell your version of the case. You will have an opportunity to do so later in the trial. Don't show you are angry. Be smart, and be prepared.
7	Prosecutor calls and questions each witness. Defendant (you) cross-examines each witness in turn.
8	The prosecution has presented all witnesses and evidence and ends, or rests its case. The prosecutor will say "the State rests."

9   The defendant (you) makes his or her opening statement or argument (optional). If you do not feel the prosecution has proven his or her case, you can make a motion for a "directed Verdict of Not Guilty." The judge will rule on your motion. If he or she agrees (sustains), the case will be over and you will be found Not Guilty. If the judge overrules (disagrees with) your motion the trial will move on to the next step.

10   The defendant (you) calls and questions his or her first witness. If you choose to testify on your own behalf, remember the prosecutor will have an opportunity to cross-examine you. You are not required to testify and cannot be compelled (required) to testify. Not testifying cannot be held against you by the judge or jury members.

11   The prosecutor cross-examines (questions) your first witness.

12   The defendant (you) calls and questions each witness you have. The prosecutor cross-examines each one. When you have finished your case and called all your witnesses, you need to tell the judge that "the defense rests."

13   The judge reads to the jury the law to be applied on the case (omit if no jury).

14   Closing arguments. The prosecutor has the right to go first and/or last. If he or she "reserves to the last," you will go first. This is your conclusion, your summation, of anything that has been said from the witness stand. Don't try to add new testimony during your closing. That time is over. Only evidence given from the witness stand by witnesses can be considered. If the prosecution goes first, you, the defendant, go last. Sometimes the prosecution is given a couple minutes of rebuttal time after you close.

15   The jury retires to consider its Verdict (omit if no jury).

16   The judge gives his or her "Judgment" or a jury renders its "Verdict."

Special Note: The "complaint" on a Class C misdemeanor filed against you as a defendant must, by law, have certain things listed in it. If you are going to court, no matter if it is a ticket or a higher charge, it is to your benefit to request a copy and read it. You may request a copy any time before the trial starts but can only object to it being "defective" twenty-four hours before the trial. Know what the requirements are for the complaint. (Look up and read Article 45.019 of the Texas Code of Criminal Procedure.)

In common language, they are:

- It must be in writing;
- it must start with "In the name and by the authority of the State of Texas";
- it must state the name of the accused (the Defendant or wrongdoer) if known, or if unknown, have a reasonable description;
- it must show that the accused has committed an offense against the law, or that the Affiant (usually a police officer) has good reason to believe and does believe the accused committed an offense against the law;
- it must include the date of the offense;
- it must have the Affiant's signature;
- it must end with the words "against the peace and dignity of the State";
- and if the charge is a city ordinance it must end with the words "contrary to the said ordinance."

3.29. Appeals

Appeals of a Guilty judgment or verdict from the justice court and most cases from a municipal court go to the county court for a new trial. Appeals must be filed within ten days of the day a Guilty judgment or verdict is made. An appeal bond is usually required.

3.30. When Most Tickets Are Given

Just so you know, most tickets are given between 11:00 p.m. and 5:00 a.m.

True Story

Steven Anyone is driving his car late at night. The streets are quiet, with almost no traffic. In fact, only one other vehicle is around. Steven has a red light as he approaches the intersection. He gets in the far right lane to make a right turn. He glances at the other car, sees that it is far enough away for safety, and only slows his car before turning, rather than stopping completely.

You guessed it. That other car was the police. The red and blues go on. Steven, remembering what happened with his motorcycle, stops immediately. This time he is going to be smart and keep trouble to the minimum. He gives the officer his driver's license and proof of insurance, as requested. While Steven is waiting for the ticket, he says nothing, but his thoughts are boiling. He's thinking how stupid this all is. He could have avoided a ticket and fine by coming to a complete stop. It would have been so easy. The few seconds saved by not stopping aren't worth the fine. What will the ticket do to his insurance? He's really kicking himself mentally.

The officer gives him the ticket to sign. He does so and returns the pad to the officer. The officer gives Steven his copy of the ticket and starts to walk away.

Steven can't hold it in any longer. He starts cursing, mad at himself, the whole situation, and maybe a little mad at the officer. The officer hears it and doesn't like it. The officer assumes it is all directed at him. Now, he's mad, too.

He arrests Steven for "Disorderly Conduct" because of his vulgar language in a public place. Steven goes directly to jail. Now Steven is really mad at himself. This Disorderly Conduct charge carries a fine of up to $500. The worst part is being arrested and jailed. To get out of jail, Steven must plead Guilty and pay the fine (giving himself a criminal record) or plead Not Guilty and pay a bail bondsman to get out. Then he must ask for a trial or plead Guilty and pay a fine. The time in jail is worse than the expense. Once again, Steven is sadder, much poorer, but, hopefully, a little wiser.

3.31. Tickets in Other States

In times past, you could ignore a ticket you were given in another state. No longer. We all have computers now. Most states are now members of the Interstate Compact. This means, if you ignore the ticket, the other state will contact your home state. Your home state may notify you at the address on your driver's license. But if you don't resolve the out-of-state ticket, your license WILL BE SUSPENDED! As a practical matter, this means you have to pay the ticket, especially since it may be very difficult to return for trial. DSC does not work for an out-of-state ticket.

Traffic Crashes

If you drive, sooner or later, you'll be involved in a crash. Most are minor with only property damage and no injuries. They can still be a pain to deal with, especially if you've never dealt with one before. Here is some basic information on how the system works.

3.32. Stop!

The first rule in any crash is to STOP. DO NOT leave the scene. The law requires that you stay. Failure to do so can result in a fine of up to $200, if property damage is less than $200. If property damage is more than $200, the fine is $0 to $2,000, and maybe even some jail time. Leaving, if there is a death, is a felony, punishable by imprisonment not to exceed five years or jail time not to exceed one year and/or a fine not to exceed $5,000. A mature person accepts the consequences of his or her actions, even if they are painful.

It is much worse to hit and run than it is just to stop after the hit.

3.33. Moving the Vehicles

Ideally, you should not move the vehicles. The investigating officer can then see the actual scene to determine fault. In the real world, this may not be practical, and in some larger cities, you must drive, pull, or push them from the roadway. If you can leave the cars where they are, pull that phone out of your pocket, and snap some pictures, it wouldn't be a bad idea. Only do so if you can safely though.

The law requires if an accident occurs on a freeway, you should move to the nearest off-ramp or service road if possible.

3.34. Warning! Warning! Warning!

When driving past an accident scene, be especially careful. It is only human to want to look and see what happened, but it is very dangerous. Everyone is looking at the scene instead of paying attention to his or her own driving. You don't want to have a crash while gawking at one that has already happened.

Special Note: If you see an accident or a police car on the side of the road with its overhead lights on, the law actually requires that you move over one lane or reduce your speed to 20 mph less than the speed limit.

3.35. To Call or Not to Call the Police

State law requires that the officers be called in any crash where anyone is hurt or killed or if the cars cannot be driven away. Violation of this law results in a ticket with a fine of up to $200.

State law requires that if you do not call the police, but anyone was hurt or killed or property damage was more than $500, you must file a written accident report with the Texas Department of Public Safety (DPS) within 10 days of the accident. Failure to do so can result in another fine of up to $200.

When in doubt, play it safe—call the police. Agreeing with the other party not to call means nothing. If the other party gets cold feet and calls the police later, you may be charged for "Leaving the Scene." *You cannot agree to break the law*.

It is easier to collect damages if the officers were called and gave the other party a ticket for causing the accident.

True Story

Steven Anyone stops at a stoplight, waiting for it to turn green. While it is still red, a car plows into him from the rear. Mr. Careless Driver jumps out of his car and apologizes. He says that it was entirely his fault (true) and that his insurance will pay for everything (also true). The damage is not too great, and no one is hurt. Mr. Driver gives Steven all kinds of information, including name, address, insurance company information, and so forth. Then Mr. Driver says, "Let's not call the cops. We'll have to wait forever." (Besides, Mr. Driver will surely be given a ticket for "Following too Closely.")

Steven agrees. Later, Steven begins to worry. What if Mr. Driver's insurance won't pay because the officers weren't called? (Not ever true!) In a panic, Steven decides to report the accident himself, several days late. An officer comes to the house to get the details. He asks Steven how much damage was done to his car. Steven says $600. Since it was more than $500, the officer promptly gives Steven a ticket for "Leaving the Scene of an Accident" without reporting it. He then locates Mr. Driver and gives him the same ticket, plus one for "Following too Closely."

It's always better to call the officers to the scene rather than call them later.

3.36. Private Property

In spite of what you have heard, police CAN investigate a traffic accident that occurs on private property if that private property is used by the general public—this means parking lots at malls, grocery stores, and shopping centers—but not private driveways.

3.37. Insurance Company Myth

Some people believe that if you don't call the officers to the crash scene, you can't collect on your insurance. WRONG! You can collect from an insurance company whether the police make a "crash report" or not. It is still better to call the officers. Insurance companies urge you to obey the law.

3.38. Get the Names of Witnesses

In some accidents, witnesses are crucial in determining fault. The best witness is someone who is a stranger to both parties in a good position to see the crash. Ideally, the officer will get the names of witnesses. Some witnesses won't want to wait for the officer, or the officer may get busy and not get the information. Don't take a chance. Get witnesses' names, addresses, and phone numbers yourself. Witnesses in your own car are better than none. However, they will be considered likely to favor you. Their testimony is not as valuable as that of a stranger.

3.39. Two Separate Legal Actions

Two separate legal actions arise from a traffic crash. One is the ticket itself, a "criminal" matter; the other is the civil matter of responsibility for the damages that have occurred. This is called "liability." The two matters are independent and separate from each other, but the ticket may have some bearing on who pays for damages.

3.40. Who's at Fault?

The officer will ask questions, look at the crash scene, and make a decision. If the officer is able to determine fault, he or she will give a ticket. If the officer is not able to determine fault (such as in traffic light cases when each party claims a green light and there are no witnesses), he or she will give no ticket. The lack of a ticket DOES NOT necessarily mean there was no fault or equal fault. It usually means that the officer simply can't tell. Determination of fault is now up to insurance companies or the courts.

Special Note: Failure to receive a ticket does not necessarily mean you don't have to pay the other party's damages.

The "Criminal" Matter of a Vehicle Accident or Crash

3.41. Accident Tickets

You were given the ticket for the majority of the fault, such as "Failure to Yield Right of Way." What do you do now? Remember, if you plead Guilty, you admit 100 percent fault. If you plead No Contest, you admit no percentage of fault. This leaves your insurance company free to determine what percentage of fault you had.

Because the stakes are high on an accident ticket (not just a fine, but a likelihood of having to pay civil damages to the other person involved), you could maximize your chances of winning by having a lawyer to defend you on the violation. Remember, the court that hears the trial on the ticket decides ONLY if you are guilty on the charge on the ticket. This court has NOTHING to do with deciding damages. The only penalty this court can impose is a fine of up to $200 payable to the State of Texas. HOWEVER, a finding of guilt by this court makes it more likely that you will pay damages to the other party. A finding of Not Guilty DOES NOT necessarily mean that you don't have to pay the other party. Damages to the other party are a civil matter.

3.42. Offsetting Penalties

Unlike football, fault on each side DOES NOT mean that each side pays his or her own damages (unless the fault is fifty–fifty). Just because the other party was speeding when you ran the stop sign does not mean that the fault is equal. The primary fault is still yours. You will still be given the ticket. In the above situation, the officer will usually give only one ticket—to the person with the most fault.

3.43. Crash Report

If a ticket was issued at the crash scene, you can get a copy of the crash report from the law enforcement agency that wrote the report. This can be done in person or by mail for a small fee several days after the crash. Insurance companies rely heavily on this report, so you should know what it says. It also gives handy information like name of the car owner, insurance company, addresses, and so forth of all parties involved.

Correcting the Crash Report: If there are mistakes on the crash report, you must contact the officer that wrote the report for any changes. If you disagree with how the officer says the crash happened and you got a chance to tell the officer your version at the scene, you are unlikely to be able to get him or her to change it now. If undisputed facts are wrong, he or she may agree to change the report. If he or she doesn't, you can only tell the insurance company your version and hope they'll believe you.

The "Civil" Matter of a Vehicle Accident or Crash

3.44. Comparative Negligence

Texas recognizes that in any given crash, no one party may be 100 percent at fault. There can be, and often is, shared fault. Who has what percentage of fault is usually determined by insurance companies or the courts. This means an insurance company for the other party may decide you had 20 percent of the fault, while their insured had 80 percent. They will then offer you 80 percent of your damages. If you accept, you pay the remaining 20 percent yourself. If you do not accept, you may have to file on your own insurance or sue the other party.

3.45. Contact the Insurance Company

If you are at fault, call your agent or the company claims office to report the crash. Let the other party know you have done so. Normally, your company will contact the other party and you will not need to have further involvement with the other party. If you have collision or PIP coverage, you will continue to deal with your insurance company for your own damages or injuries.

If you are the innocent party, wait a day or so for the at-fault party or his or her insurance company to call you. If you don't hear from anyone, take action. You can call the at-fault party or call directly to his or her insurance company. Those accidents with injuries or an undrivable car usually get faster treatment. Be patient, be polite, but be persistent. If the insurance company claims agent is to call you back, find out when. If the call does not come on time, promptly call back. Remember, the squeaking wheel gets the grease, or the persistent get prompter attention.

3.46. Amount You Are Entitled to Receive in Damages

Nobody comes out ahead after a crash, even the party who was not at fault. Under Texas law, the measure of damages is the cost of repair, until that cost is greater than the value of the vehicle. That means, if the cost of repair is $2,000, but your car is worth only $1,500, the at-fault party is responsible for paying you only $1,500. This is called a "total." Even though the $1,500 may not get you as good a car as you had before the crash, all you are entitled to is $1,500. You cannot go back and sue the at-fault party for more.

Special Note: In a total, you give the title to your "totaled" car to the insurance company, which pays you the $1,500. The company is entitled to get the salvage value, if any. If you want to keep your car and add your own money to the insurance money to get it fixed, negotiate this with the insurance company. They will probably do it but will pay you only the $1,500 minus the salvage value, if any.

3.47. How the System Works

1. The insurance company is notified of the accident.
2. An adjustor and/or claims agent is assigned the case. The claims agent works directly for the insurance company. The adjustor works either directly for the insurance company or for an independent adjusting company that has been hired by the insurance company.

3. Either the claims agent or adjustor takes your statement about the accident over the phone. Don't panic because it is being recorded. Just get the facts straight in your mind so that the recording makes sense.

4. The adjustor looks at your car and estimates the damages. He or she determines if it can be repaired or if it is a total.

   Special Note: Sometimes, if the damage is slight, you may be asked to get estimates to send to the insurance company, rather than an adjustor actually viewing your car.

5. If your car can be repaired, you get a rental car from the insurance company while your car is being repaired or while your car cannot be driven. If you are claiming on your own insurance rather than the other party's insurance, check your policy. You may not have coverage that provides a rental car. If your car is TOTALED, you are NOT ENTITLED to a rental car.

6. You choose the body shop for your repairs.

7. The car is repaired.

8. The check for the repair is made out to the body shop and you or just to you. You endorse the check.

9. You will also be asked to sign a "waiver of liability." This means that you agree that the at-fault party DOES NOT legally owe you any more money for car repair. It is printed either on the back of the check or maybe on a separate piece of paper. Usually, you MUST sign this to get the money to pay for the repair of your car.

   Special Note 1: Remember, this waiver covers property damage only. It has nothing to do with any medical reimbursement you are owed for injuries, so it is okay to sign it, even though all of your medical has not yet been paid.

   Special Note 2: After you sign the waiver, if the body shop finds additional damage from the accident that was missed by the adjustor, the insurance company WILL STILL PAY for it, even though you have signed the waiver. Have the body shop call the adjustor or insurance company directly to explain.

3.48. You Disagree with the Amount Offered

This usually occurs in two situations:

1. Percentage of fault: As noted previously, there can be shared fault in a crash. You may disagree with the at-fault party's insurance company that you were 20 percent at fault in the accident. If so, attempt to negotiate. If negotiation fails, you can refuse the offer to pay 80 percent of your damages. Then you claim on your own insurance for full payment minus deductible, if you have collision coverage. Your insurance company then attempts to collect. If you do not have collision coverage, you can sue the at-fault party in court and let a jury decide if you were 20 percent at fault. More about suing later.

2. Value of your car: The insurance company agrees that their insured was 100 percent at fault. They say your car is "totaled." They offer you $2,000 for your car. You think your car is worth more than that. First check "book value." Look it up online or call the dealer for your make and model, and ask the dealer to give you "book value." If your car is older, its condition prior to the accident and the number of miles on it make a difference in value. If book value is unavailable or too low, ask used-car dealers what they would have bought such a car for and then how much they would have marked it up to sell it. An average of those two figures can be used as fair market value. Armed with this information, you may be able to convince the insurance company that your car is worth more than they offered. If not, again you can claim on your own insurance or file suit in court.

3.49. Medical Bills

If the other party was at fault and had insurance, all of your medical bills should be paid for you. If you must pay up front at the emergency room, get a receipt so that you can be reimbursed later.

Some insurance companies prefer that you have bills sent directly to them for payment. Some let you pay and then reimburse you. Negotiate the method of payment, if possible.

You can settle the car damage quickly and wait on the medical. Most insurance companies expect to wait to settle the medical until your doctor releases you. If the doctor releases you but says you might need more surgery in a year, you can negotiate that with the insurance company. They'll handle it one of two ways. Either they'll simply wait to close that part of the claim until the time has passed, or they'll offer you a written agreement in which they'll agree to pay for all reasonable medical expenses arising from your injury for a set period of time. If you are not happy with the agreement offered, then you can file on your own insurance or file suit.

Special Note: If you are at fault in the accident, remember that your car insurance policy covers your medical only if you have PIP coverage. PIP also covers your passengers. If you do not have PIP coverage, you must claim on your medical insurance policy. If your passenger is not covered on your medical policy and there is no PIP, your passenger must claim on her or his own medical insurance policy. If the passenger doesn't have such a policy, the passenger can sue you and be covered under your liability policy.

3.50. Medical Payments If At-Fault Party Is Uninsured

If you have uninsured motorist coverage, you can claim on that for both property damage and medical payments. If you do NOT have this coverage, you must claim on your own medical insurance.

3.51. Other Expenses

If the other party is at fault, you may claim for such out-of-pocket expenses as lost wages, damaged clothing, eyeglasses, and items damaged in the car, like school books or a laptop. If you are at fault and claiming on your own insurance, you are not likely to be reimbursed for these expenses.

3.52. "Pain and Suffering"

This term is used to refer to the aggravation, discomfort, inconvenience, and pain that you have when you have AN INJURY. It is difficult to recover any money under this if you were not injured.

How much is fair? Good question. It depends on the type of injury and how painful or disabling it was.

You can negotiate this with the insurance company or hire a lawyer to negotiate for you.

3.53. If the At-Fault Party Refuses to File on His or Her Insurance

Nobody can make the at-fault party file. If the innocent party is not happy with how the at-fault party is willing to pay or if the at-fault party refuses to pay, the innocent party can sue. The insurance company of the at-fault party WILL NOT be involved in the suit at all. The company will provide no lawyer to defend and will pay no damages awarded. The at-fault party is on his or her own if he or she refuses to file the claim with the insurance company in the beginning.

If you think you are not at fault in the crash, but the other party thinks you are, it is far better to let your insurance company process the claim. If the company agrees with you and refuses to pay the other party, the company will provide a lawyer to defend you and pay any damages awarded (up to the policy limits) if you lose the lawsuit.

Special Note: If the at-fault party intends to pay on his or her own, he or she can do so. The innocent party DOES NOT have to accept installments, unless ordered to do so by a court judgment. If the innocent party claims on his or her uninsured motorist coverage, the insurance company will seek to collect from the at-fault party. The company may be willing to accept installments.

3.54. Uninsured Motorist

If the uninsured motorist is at fault, the uninsured motorist owes the damages himself or herself. If the uninsured motorist is unable or refuses to pay, the innocent party can claim on his or her own insurance or sue.

3.55. If You Claim on Your Own Uninsured Motorist Coverage, Can You Sue the At-Fault Uninsured Motorist to Collect Your Deductible?

No! Once you claim on your insurance for any amount, you give up your right to sue the at-fault party to the insurance company. This is called "subrogation." The insurance company will go after the at-fault party for their own money plus your deductible. If they ever recover it, you'll get reimbursed. If they are unable to recover it, you're just out the money. If your insurance company decides NOT TO SUE the at-fault party, you may be able to get permission in writing to sue the at-fault party from your insurance company. Then you can sue for your deductible in the small claims court. You may win your suit but may never be able to collect the money (see § 8.11 on small claims court for further information).

3.56. Suing the Other Party

Currently, if the amount of damage is less than $10,000, you can file suit by yourself without a lawyer in small claims court. (This $10,000 amount is being discussed in current session of the legislature and may be raised.) The filing fee can be an amount up to seventy-five dollars. Either party can bring a lawyer to small claims court if he or she is willing to pay for one (see § 8.11 for more details).

For amounts over $10,000, you must file in a county or district court, which is very difficult to do without a lawyer.

The disadvantage to suing is that it costs money and may take some time. Collecting the judgment from an uninsured party can be very difficult. Suits must be filed within two years of the date of the accident.

3.57. Do You Need a Lawyer?

It depends. Generally speaking, the more serious the accident, the more likely that you need a lawyer. Lawyers can negotiate for you with the other party's insurance company. Lawyers can file suit, if necessary. If you are claiming on your own insurance, you will generally not need a lawyer.

3.58. License Suspension

One threat that you have to compel a person to pay you is license suspension and car registration suspension. If anyone was killed or injured or more than $1,000 worth of property damage occurred, and the at-fault party won't pay, you can file with the DPS to have his or her license suspended and car license tags removed. You can do this before you file suit. This suspension lasts two years from the date of the crash, unless you file suit by that time. If you file suit for any amount of damages and win, the suspension lasts until you are paid.

To do this, contact your local DPS office for instructions. Of course, if you lose your suit and the other party is found not at fault, the suspension ends.

3.59. If You're Driving Someone Else's Car and Are at Fault

The car owner's insurance will pay any innocent parties. The insurance company then will come to you for reimbursement. If you are insured, your own policy will pay. If you are not, you owe the money yourself.

3.60. Policy Limits

The insurance company is only liable (responsible) up to the policy limits. If the at-fault party is insured only at the state limits of 20/40/15 and your injuries are $25,000, the at-fault party is personally responsible for the remaining $5,000.

This is why it is recommended that you carry more than the minimum insurance.

Special Note: If you sue, you always sue the party at fault, not his or her insurance company.

Chapter 4

PRANKS, CRIMES, AND ARREST

You have seen many things done on YouTube, television, or in the movies that are shown as funny pranks or harmless fun. Nobody seems to ever get hurt or into any real trouble. It's all presented as a big joke. But *this is real life*.

In real life, many of those "funny pranks" are CRIMES. Crimes lead to punishment that few people ever find funny. KNOW BEFORE YOU ACT, and avoid nasty surprises.

Classification of Crimes

Below are the classifications of *most* criminal offenses and the name of the court that would try (or handle) the case. See the following diagram for further information on the appeal process.

Municipal Court or Justice of the Peace Court:
    Class C misdemeanor

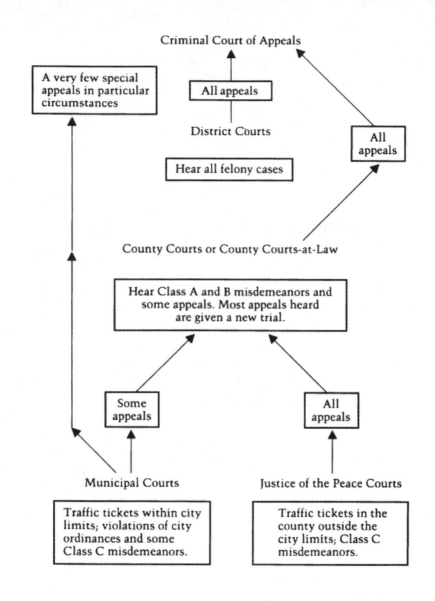

County Court or County Court-at-Law:
   Class B misdemeanor
   Class A misdemeanor
District Court:
   State Jail felony
   Third-degree felony
   Second-degree felony
   First-degree felony
   Capital felony
*Texas Court of Criminal Appeals (The state's court of last resort
   for criminal cases)*:
   All appeals from the District Courts of Texas
   All appeals from the county or county courts-at-law in Texas
   A few specific appeals from municipal courts in Texas
Texas Supreme Court:
   Final court for all appealed civil cases
   Authority to determine certain legal matters over which
      no other court has jurisdiction. (We will not discuss
      these here.)

The Truth about Arrest and Jail

4.1. Being Read Your Rights

On TV, as the officer fastens the handcuffs, he or she reads you your "rights." In real life, it doesn't happen that way.

Your "rights," called the Miranda warning, state that you don't have to answer questions, that you have the right to talk to an attorney (lawyer) before being questioned by the police, and that an attorney will be appointed for you if you can't afford one. Further detail on the Miranda warning will be given later in this chapter.

As a citizen, or anyone in the United States of America, you have certain rights, and they can never be taken away. In an encounter with a police officer, the officer may read your rights to you, or he or she may not. If you are being charged with a crime your rights WILL always be read to you at one point or another. If you are being charged with a crime, sometimes the officer will want to get a statement from you. "A statement" is your version of what happened and what role you played in the crime. If you are sixteen or younger, before the officer can take your statement, you must be taken to a place designated by the district judge of your area called a "Juvenile Processing Office." In this office, and *only* in this office, can a juvenile (person younger than seventeen years of age) be questioned, fingerprinted, photographed, or temporarily detained or give a statement. The officer will have to move fast because, by law, he or she only has six hours to get the process completed when dealing with a juvenile.

If the police officer wants a statement from you, he or she must call in a "magistrate." A magistrate is normally a judge, but he or she is seldom the judge that will decide guilt or innocence in your case. The magistrate's job, in this scenario, is to read and explain your rights to you. This is called a "juvenile warning." It will be just you and the magistrate in the Juvenile Processing Office, unless YOU ask for your parents or an attorney. Your parents can hoot and holler in the lobby of the police station and nothing will change. You, and only you, are the one that has to ask for them to be there. Remember, the magistrate is not there to decide if you are guilty or not. He or she is just there to make sure everything is done correctly and by the law. The magistrate will explain the process and begin by reading you your rights. Make sure if you have questions you *ASK THEM*! Now is *NOT* the time to act like the smartest person in the room that knows it all.

Let's go through your rights and break each of them down.

YOU MAY REMAIN SILENT AND NOT MAKE ANY STATEMENT AT ALL.

A lot of young people, for one reason or another, seem to think this means "don't speak until spoken to," but that is not what it means at all. It means, when the magistrate is finished with the juvenile warning (explaining all your rights), he or she will step out and a police officer will step in to take your statement. You DO NOT have to talk to the officer if you don't want to. You have the right to simply tell the officer, "I don't want to talk" or "I don't want to give a statement."

Please don't think this means you don't have to talk to the magistrate. Remember, the magistrate is there to make sure that everything is done according to the law, and he or she must know that you understand ALL of your rights.

ANY STATEMENT YOU MAKE MAY BE USED AS EVIDENCE AGAINST YOU.

If you do choose to talk to the officer, what you say will either be written down or video recorded. Again, what you say is considered "your statement." It is your version of what happened and the role you played. If in your statement you confess to a crime and that crime is taken to trial in a court, what you said can be played or read in court. If you confess, your written- or video-recorded confession will be used as evidence against you at your trial. Just like a fingerprint on the trigger of a weapon used in a shooting, your statement is evidence.

YOU HAVE THE RIGHT TO HAVE AN ATTORNEY PRESENT TO ADVISE YOU EITHER PRIOR TO ANY QUESTIONING OR DURING ANY QUESTIONING.

Let's define a few words before we cover what the whole sentence means. What's an attorney? An attorney is another name for a lawyer. A lawyer is someone who has studied and is an expert in the LAW.

Let's keep moving. You have the right to have an *expert in the law* . . . present to advise you. "Present" means "with you" and "to advise you" means "to give you advice." The last word that is a little strange is the word "prior" and prior means "before." When we break the whole thing down it is really not that difficult to understand.

The whole sentence means: *You have the right to have an expert in the law with you, to give you advice, before or when you are answering any questions by the police.*

IF YOU ARE UNABLE TO EMPLOY AN ATTORNEY, YOU HAVE THE RIGHT TO HAVE AN ATTORNEY APPOINTED TO ADVISE YOU BEFORE OR DURING ANY QUESTIONING AND INTERVIEWS WITH PEACE OFFICERS OR ATTORNEYS REPRESENTING THE STATE.

This one is a lot like the one above, so you already know what the gist is. Let's break this one down too. "If you are unable to employ an attorney" means that you have the right to have an attorney appointed even if you cannot afford one. What does that mean? "Appointed" means "assigned" or "given to." That means the State of Texas will pay for the attorney if you can't. Keep in mind, because you are a juvenile and your parents are ultimately responsible for you, the court may require them to pay for your attorney. Your parents or guardians may have to file paperwork stating they can't afford one either, if that is the case. A "peace officer" is a legal name for a police officer, and an "attorney representing the state" is the lawyer working with the police, that will present a case *against* you if your case goes to a trial. Both of them, the police and the attorney representing the state, are the other side if you are charged with a crime.

The whole thing: *If you cannot afford an expert in the law, you have the right to have an expert in the law given to or provided for you, paid for by the State of Texas, and he or she will give you advice before or when you are talking to police officers or any attorney that may bring charges against you.*

Whew! Let's move to the last one. It's an easy one.

YOU HAVE THE RIGHT TO TERMINATE THE INTERVIEW AT ANY TIME.

Remember the old movie *The Terminator*? The Terminator was sent back in time to STOP a woman from giving birth to a son that would one day lead a revolution against the machines. His whole purpose was to STOP her. That's right. "Terminate" means to stop. *You have the right to STOP the interview at any time.* If after you are read and explained your rights you decide to speak with a police officer and give a statement, you can stop, at any time. It may be tough to tell a police officer you are done, but remember you have the right to do just that.

Special Note: We started this section with the importance of, if you are taken into custody, you should be asking questions and probably a lot of them. After this brief explanation of your legal rights, you may feel a bit more comfortable. But if you are ever in the situation where a magistrate is sitting across the table from you, this book will be the furthest thing from your mind. ASK QUESTIONS and keep asking until you understand.

After you have either given the police officer your statement or told him or her that you don't want to talk, the magistrate will enter the room once again. This time he or she will ask several questions about you. The questions will range from how old you are to how far you have gone in school to how the officers have treated you while you have been with them. Be honest. Again, the magistrate is there to make sure everything is done according to the law. If you do give a statement and that statement was written down, the magistrate will read it to you to verify that it is what you said, meant to say, and wanted to say. Pay attention. You will sign off on each page proving that those are your words and you want to stick to them.

4.2. You Are an Adult at Age Seventeen If You Commit a Crime

For the purpose of committing a crime, currently, you are treated as an adult at age seventeen in Texas. Every legislative session this is debated in congress but for now that means you can be given the full punishment allowed by law at seventeen. For every other purpose, except drinking alcohol, you are treated as an adult at age eighteen. As you know, to buy and drink alcohol legally, you must be twenty-one or in the company of your parents or your twenty-one-year-old or older spouse.

At seventeen or older, the rights explained in § 4.1 still apply to you. The difference is at seventeen you can be arrested, jailed, and, no matter how many times you ask, mom does not get to be with you. You will still see a magistrate, and he or she will still read and explain your rights to you. Just later in the process. Just because you have had that seventeenth birthday and are sitting in a concrete building with no windows doesn't mean you can't ask questions. When you do see a magistrate, he or she will answer any question you may have, but again, you'd better stay polite.

4.3. What Really Happens If You Are Arrested and Jailed

Whether you are arrested on traffic-ticket warrants or for murder, at seventeen or older, the process is basically the same.

1. Handcuffs: Most officers use them on ALL offenders, even women, regardless of the reason for the arrest. They are used for the officer's protection. They are frequently fastened tight enough to leave marks on your wrists when they are removed. That is not illegal.
2. Treatment: People complain, "I'm being treated like a criminal." Once arrested, regardless of what the arrest was for, you will be treated the same as everyone else. The officers or jailers may not be polite, and your handling may not be gentle. They usually take the lead from you and your actions.
3. Mug shots and fingerprints: These are taken of all people jailed, regardless of the charge. Keep in mind, with the internet, those mug shots never go away.
4. Searches: I mean searches of your person. The officer who initially stops you can do a pat-down search of you for weapons. If arrested, when at the jail, a *thorough* search of you is done before you are put in a cell. Understand the definition of the word "thorough"? Every nook and cranny will be searched.
5. Phone call: You have the legal right to one phone call. You'll make it at the jailor's convenience, not yours. You may get to make it right away, or it may be hours later. Use your call to at least let your parents know where you are (they always worry) and preferably to arrange bail money to get out. Some jails have payphones in the holding cells. These phones are almost always for collect calls only.
6. Holding cells: Jails don't have a special cell for traffic offenders, college students, or young people. If you are seventeen or older, once booked in, you're put in the holding

cell with whomever else has been recently arrested. On TV, the holding cell is never crowded, and the other prisoners are asleep or friendly. In reality, most jails are crowded, there are no empty bunks, it is very cold, and your fellow prisoners are not pleasant to smell or talk to.

7. Magistration: You will almost always see a magistrate at the jail. This magistration hearing is your first court hearing and sometimes is referred to in the slang term "arraignment." This hearing must be held within twenty-four hours after arrest on a misdemeanor or within forty-eight hours of arrest on a felony. In this hearing, a magistrate will read and determine probable cause in your case. If he or she finds probable cause, you will be read and explained your rights and told what the charge is. The magistrate typically will ask several questions regarding your financial status. This is not done to pry into your life but to determine how much bond will be placed on you for your case. Bond cannot be punitive. Meaning it isn't set to punish you. Bond is set to make sure you make it to all your court hearings. Too low and you may not take it seriously and skip court. Too high and you may not be able to make bond, and you will have to sit in jail until your trial. Answering the questions of the magistrate as specifically as possible is to your benefit.

Special Note 1: During this magistration hearing, you will also be asked if you can afford an attorney to handle your case. You can always take the paperwork and decide at a later time to hire your own attorney. Also, don't expect your parents to fork out the money for your attorney. If they choose to do so, great. But keep in mind, your parents are not typically the reason you are in the spot you are. You should share with your parents the circumstances, but don't get angry if they choose to let you suffer the consequences of your actions.

Special Note 2: The magistrate will also ask if you are a citizen of the United States. If you are not a citizen, you will be given the opportunity to decide if you would like your home country's consulate to be notified. On your say-so only will the jail staff notify your home country of where you are being held and what charge you are being held on.

8. Length of detention after bond is made or fine paid: The courts have allowed at least twenty-four hours. You're released at the jail's convenience, not yours. Your actions usually set the speed of the jailors releasing you.

   Special Note: If you are arrested for Driving While Intoxicated (DWI) or an assault on a family member, you will be held at least four hours, regardless of when bail is posted.

True Story

Remember when Steven got arrested for cursing the officer? After he bonded out of jail, Steven went to see his attorney.

After telling his version of what happened, Steven wails, "You won't believe where they put me. I thought jails were segregated."

His lawyer blinks and thinks, "Hasn't this guy ever heard of the civil rights movement? Surely he doesn't mean racially segregated."

The lawyer asks Steven, "Do you mean racially segregated?" Steven says, "No, no, no. Not that. I mean they put me in with the criminals."

Puzzled, the lawyer says, "Where did you expect them to put you?" Steven says, "Don't they have a separate cell for college students?" The lawyer nearly dies laughing.

No, there is no separate cell for young people over sixteen years of age, for traffic offenders, or for college students. You get thrown in the tank with anyone else recently arrested.

4.4. How to Get Out of Jail

1. Pay the fine: *If you are charged with a Class C misdemeanor* and the fine is already set, you can pay the money, usually by money order, and be released. What you have done is paid a *cash*

bond (explained in the next section). With a cash bond, you have a couple of different options. You can contact the court within ten days (in person) and request a court date, a payment plan, or community service. If you wait until day eleven, you are too late. The cash bond you posted, at the jail, will be used to pay the fine, and you will get the conviction for the charge.

Again, if you post a cash bond, at the jail in the amount of the fine, and do nothing (don't contact the court), the bond will be used as the fine, and you will get the conviction for the charge. I said it twice. Hope you caught that.

Special Note: Class C misdemeanor warrants typically have preset fines. That means the judge has already set the amount of fine for all charges. Therefore, you don't have to appear before a judge to find out the amount of the fine. It will be told to you at the time of the book-in process.

If you don't have the money to post a cash bond, you will be brought before a magistrate. This may be the next day but for a Class C will always be within twenty-four hours. This is the time to ask all those questions I keep talking about. For example, "Can I get a payment plan or community service?" I have a lot of defendants that evidently feel they have more time than money and ask if they can just "lay out" the fines. This means they would rather sit in jail until the fine is taken care of. Some judges will allow this, and some will not, thinking it is an added cost to the city or county for feeding and housing yet another inmate. If the request is made to *sit out the fine* and it is granted by the court, how much of the fine you are credited with per day varies from county to county.

IMPORTANT! You always have an opportunity to request a hearing to explain your financial status. This is called an "Indigency Hearing." The Texas Constitution, article 1, section 18, tells us, "No person shall ever be imprisoned for debt." You cannot be jailed because you are simply too poor to pay your fine. TELL THE JUDGE OR MAGISTRATE, AND REQUEST A HEARING. This scenario is only for a Class C misdemeanors.

If you plead "Not Guilty" to a Class C misdemeanor or are charged with a higher misdemeanor (Class B or A) or any felony offense, the following are your options after your magistrate's hearing and a bond has been set.

2. Post the bond: A bond is a guarantee or promise that you won't skip town and ignore your trial date. The different types of bond include:

   a) Personal Recognizance bond (PR bond): You sign a paper bond in which you promise to appear for all court appearances when so ordered. Your signature is the guarantee that you will appear. It is your word or promise. A judge must approve this type of bond. If your offense is not serious and people know you and affirm your reliability, then you may get one. Always ask. It never hurts to ask. If you fail to appear when you are supposed to, a warrant is issued for your arrest, and you owe the amount of the bond to the state. Oh, and you shouldn't expect to ever get another PR bond.

   b) Cash bond (written about above for Class C misdemeanors): If the magistrate has set the bond at $1,000, you, or a friend or family member, can pay $1,000 cash, or a $1,000 money order, to the sheriff's escrow account to guarantee you'll appear for all court appearances. If you fail to appear, the money is forfeited, and a warrant for your arrest is issued. If you appear as ordered, make it to all your court hearings, and your case is completed, YOU GET BACK THE CASH IN FULL, but without interest. This is the cheapest way to go, if you can come up with the cash.

   c) Bond through an attorney: Some attorneys will guarantee your promise to appear for all court appearances with a paper bond. The paper bond does not require you to pay cash for the bond amount, UNLESS you skip town. ONLY A FEW ATTORNEYS DO THIS and usually only if they already know you. The attorney may charge a fee for this guarantee, over and above his or her regular legal fee. If you do not appear, a warrant is issued for your arrest, and you owe the state the amount of the bond. You will probably have to find a new attorney, too.

d) Bail bond (most common): Most people use this because no PR bond was granted, they don't have enough cash to post a cash bond, and they don't know an attorney who makes attorney bonds. In this case, a nonrefundable fee is paid to a professional bail bondsman to post a paper bond for the amount of the bond. The bondsman guarantees to the court that you will show up for all court appearances. You avoid having to pay the full amount of the bond, as you do in a cash bond situation, but you don't ever get any money back. You also don't have to sit in jail. You will have to maintain close contact with the bondsman.

The amount of the fee you must pay varies from bondsman to bondsman but can range from 10 to 20 percent of the total bond set by the magistrate. From jail, it may be difficult to shop around for the cheapest. You could, and maybe should, use your phone call to notify a friend, or loved one, and ask him or her to shop around for the cheapest fee. Keep in mind, if you don't show up in court when ordered to do so, you and the bondsman owe the court the full amount of the bond, and a warrant is issued for your arrest. The bondsman also starts looking for you. It is much harder and more expensive to find a bondsman a second time if you've violated your bond the first time.

When you make bond in one of the ways described above, you get out of jail.

Special Note: If you are charged with any of the following four offenses, bail may be denied by the magistrate if:

- You are accused of a capital offense and the State of Texas presents proof that conviction and death sentence will result from the trial;
- you are accused of certain sexual offenses involving a child;

- you are accused of violating a magistrate's order of emergency protection or a protective order;
- and/or you are arrested for violating a condition of bond relating to family violence.

4.5. How Much Will the Bond Be?

A magistrate will set the amount of the bond; therefore, the amounts vary from jail to jail. Several factors are used by the magistrate to set your bond. The seriousness of the crime is one factor. Where you live in relation to where you are jailed is another. Your history of missing court is probably the most important. Remember, as stated above, your bond is not meant to punish you. Just a guarantee you will make it to court.

After Jail Comes Court—What to Expect

Special Note: In the following section, we are NOW discussing the court process that occurs after you are charged with a higher misdemeanor (B or A misdemeanor) or felony offense. The court process for Class C misdemeanors filed in a municipal court or justice of the peace court are discussed in § 3.17.

4.6. Arraignment / Magistration

This is your first appearance IN COURT before a judge that will sit over your case. It can be scheduled months after you were first arrested. If you have already hired an attorney, he or she should meet you there for this. If not, you should have your paperwork for a court-appointed attorney already filled out. More often than not, the courtroom will be full of people. With attorneys and court staff scurrying around, defendants who are out on bond, like you, and inmates in jumpsuits and chains. The whole thing can be a little scary. You should be dressed as professional as possible and sit quietly for your case to be called. You will be explained your rights, once again. The judge will tell you the charge you are being charged with and will expect a plea.

4.7. Entering a Plea on a Higher Misdemeanor or Felony

A plea of "Not Guilty" can always be changed later if you change your mind. Pleading Not Guilty allows your attorney maneuvering room to plea bargain or represent you in trial.

Pleading GUILTY OR NO CONTEST means no plea bargaining. You may get a harsher punishment, and you may have to pay a fine or spend time in jail right away.

4.8. Do You Need an Attorney?

You are allowed by law to represent yourself if you choose to do so. Be smart. Refer to the section later in this chapter on "Specific Crimes" for the chart on punishment.

4.9. Finding an Attorney

Ask family and friends for referrals. (See § 8.6 Finding and Hiring an Attorney for step-by-step help.) Your local bar association may have a referral service. The State Bar Association does have a referral service. You can call and tell the operator which city or town you are in and that you need an attorney for criminal law.

Texas Bar Association
(1-800) 252-9690
www.texasbar.com

You can shop for yourself online or by checking the phone book. Attorneys, in the phone book, will be listed alphabetically in the yellow pages under "attorney." Some attorneys will have advertisements that indicate they practice criminal law. Your best bet is to shop around and talk to several attorneys. Feeling comfortable with an attorney you choose is as important as the fee amount (for further information on choosing a lawyer, see § 8.6).

4.10. Court-Appointed Attorneys

You can ask for a court-appointed attorney at your first hearing or arraignment. You must satisfy the judge that you are too indigent (poor) to hire an attorney. If you can't afford to bond out of jail, then obviously you can't afford a lawyer. If you can afford to make bond, it is harder (but not impossible) to convince the judge that you are too poor to hire a lawyer. If you are supported by your parents while going to school or college but have no money yourself, it is difficult to convince a judge that he or she should appoint an attorney because you don't want to tell your parents what is going on. I know lots of judges and don't think you will find a judge that will have much sympathy with your desire not to tell your parents about your arrest.

A court-appointed attorney is ethically bound to do his or her best to represent you as well as a hired attorney would.

Some cities have a public defender office that represents you in these cases. In cities that don't, a private attorney will be appointed.

4.11. Plea Bargaining

During the time between your first hearing (arraignment) and trial, your attorney will attempt to bargain with the prosecuting attorney to get you the best possible deal. If an acceptable bargain is reached, you will plead Guilty in exchange for a specific punishment promised by the prosecuting attorney. Probation, deferred adjudication, or less time incarcerated may be offered. This may be best for everyone. You will save money in attorney's fees by not going to trial, and you aren't gambling on being found Guilty or what the punishment will be. The state is happy because they dispose of a case without the cost and time for a trial.

4.12. Trial

If no acceptable plea bargain is reached, or you want to go to trial, then a trial date is set. It will usually be several months, sometimes a year, before the trial. As a general rule, the more serious the crime, the longer it takes to get to trial. You can change your mind and plead Guilty any time.

If you go to trial for one of these higher charges, you should be represented by an attorney. Technically, you can represent yourself in any court, but it may not be wise to do so. Trials, at this level, are generally too complicated for a nonlawyer. The one exception to this general rule is, as stated above, on a Class C misdemeanor case.

4.13. Appeals

If for any reason you feel as if you didn't get a "fair shot" in whatever court your case was first filed, you can always appeal to the next level. The appeals process almost always requires a lawyer (see the graph at the beginning of this chapter).

Specific Crimes

The penal code and other statute books are filled with numerous crimes a person may commit. Those listed below are some that are likely to be of most interest to you. This is *not* intended as a complete list. Remember, most of these crimes lead to an arrest and jail on the day of the arrest, as well as punishment. Drug- and alcohol-related crimes will be covered in separate sections at the end of this chapter.

Degree and Punishment of Crime

Class C misdemeanor (usually a citation [ticket] but may also be by arrest)—fine only—up to $500 fine. Some fines for city ordinance or fire code violations are up to $2,000 per day.

Class B misdemeanor—up to six months in jail and/or a fine of up to $2,000.

Class A misdemeanor—up to twelve months in jail and/or a
   fine up to $4,000.
State Jail felony—six months to two years in a state jail; in
   addition, a possible fine not to exceed $10,000.
Third-degree felony—two to ten years in the penitentiary; in
   addition, a possible fine not to exceed $10,000.
Second-degree felony—two to twenty years in the penitentiary; in addition, a possible fine not to exceed $10,000.
First-degree felony—life or five to ninety-nine years in the penitentiary; in addition, a possible fine not to exceed $10,000.
Capital felony—life imprisonment or death by lethal injection.

Nonclassified crimes: There are certain other criminal offenses that
do not fall under these classifications. The punishment on these
offenses will be noted when the offense is described.

4.14. Laser Pointers

You can commit a Class C misdemeanor if you knowingly shine a laser
pointer at a uniformed safety officer; this includes police officers,
security guards, firefighters, and emergency medical service workers.
   If you intentionally shine a laser pointer at an aircraft and it
impairs the operator of that aircraft's ability to control the aircraft,
it is a Class A misdemeanor. By the way, commercial aircraft have
special cameras that track the laser to the source.

4.15. Vandalism

In the law vandalism is called "Criminal Mischief," and it means
defacing, damaging, or destroying the property of another. The
punishment is set by the value of the item destroyed or the amount
of damage done.

4.16. Graffiti

If you paint, use a permanent marker, or etch or engrave on anyone
else's property without his or her consent, you have broken the law.

This includes anything from your school desk to the side of a building. This charge can range from a Class C to a felony depending on how much damage is done. Graffiti on or within a school or church is a State Jail felony.

4.17. Abusive, Indecent, Profane, or Vulgar Language or Gestures

Use of this type of language or gesture in a public place is illegal. Your car has been ruled a "public place" if you're on a public street or highway. This is a "Disorderly Conduct" offense and is a Class C misdemeanor.

4.18. Too Much Noise

Making unreasonable noise in a public place OR near a private residence you do not occupy is a crime under the disorderly conduct statute. If the music is too loud at your party, the officers can arrest you. As the host of the party, you are responsible for the actions and noise of your guests. You may get a warning to lower the noise level, but NO WARNING IS REQUIRED. This is a Class C misdemeanor.

4.19. Mooning or Taking a Leak Outside

Exposing yourself, front or rear, in public, and being reckless about whether you are offending or alarming anyone is a CRIME. It is "Disorderly Conduct" and can range from Class C to a Class B misdemeanor.

4.20. Failure to Attend School

Even though the law on this has changed in the last few years and the "criminal" part of it has been taken away, there are still rules you have to follow and consequences if you don't. If you are twenty-one years of age or younger and have enrolled in school (at the beginning of the year), you *must* attend. Attendance means if you miss ten or more days or parts of days within a six-month period or three or more days within a four-week period you are subject to prosecution. This charge is now a "civil" case, and you can be subject to paying civil penalties . . . money.

4.21. Hazing

Yes, "Hazing" is a CRIME. Hazing consists of any intentional, knowing, or reckless act that endangers the mental or physical safety of a student, including, but not limited to:

1. Physical brutality;
2. Physical activity like sleep deprivation, exposure to weather, confinement in a small space, or calisthenics;
3. Requiring the eating or drinking of any substance that causes unreasonable risk of harm;
4. Any activity that intimidates, threatens, causes ostracism, extreme mental stress, shame, humiliation, or causes loss of dignity.

Punishment for hazing is for individuals and the organization. If an individual engages in hazing, encourages, directs, or aids hazing, knowingly permits hazing to occur, or has firsthand knowledge of hazing and fails to report it to the school, college or university, he or she is guilty of hazing.

PUNISHMENT

1. Failure to report: Class B misdemeanor
2. Everything else:
   a) No serious bodily injury—Class B misdemeanor
   b) Serious bodily injury—Class A misdemeanor
   c) Death—State Jail felony

If the organization, an officer, or any combination of members, pledges, or alumni CONDONE, ENCOURAGE, COMMIT, or ASSIST in hazing, they can be found Guilty.

1. No property damage or physical injury: fine of not less than $5,000 nor more than $10,000
2. Personal injury, property damage, or death: fine of not less than $5,000 nor more than double the amount lost or expenses incurred

Remember, CONSENT to hazing is NEVER a defense. IMMUNITY from prosecution is available to those testifying for the prosecution. Nothing prevents a school, college, or university from imposing its own punishment against the organization and individual members. In addition, if physical injury or death occurs, civil lawsuits are likely to be filed against the school or organization and its members. Don't be fooled into thinking that a prosecutor has more serious crimes to prosecute than hazing. In the recent past, both females and males have been prosecuted.

4.22. Cyberbullying

Cyberbullying is any act (even one act) by one or more students that is directed at another student and is meant to intimidate that student by using any electronic communication device. Cell phone, text, computer, email, camera, social-media app, website, or any other internet-based communication tool are all included here. This act may involve not only a physical threat, or even a fear of being harmed, but also a threat or fear of damage to the student's property.

New additions to the law on cyberbullying now cover this type of bullying whether the it occurs on or off school property, if it interferes with any student's right to an education, or if it disrupts a classroom, school, school-sponsored or school-related activity. These additions also require school districts to devise a plan to address bullying and cyberbullying. These plans can require bullies to be withdrawn from school and enrolled in Alternative Education Programs (AEP) or even expelled.

Not only may a bully be charged with a crime of harassment or assault but also a bully or his or her parents—if the bully is under eighteen-years-old—may be sued in civil court and a restraining order may be put in place (see § 5.24).

The degree of the harassment or assault charge is a Class B misdemeanor unless:

- the bullying was committed against a minor under the age of eighteen;
- the bully intended the victim to commit suicide;
- the bully's conduct caused serious bodily injury to the victim;
- or the bully had violated an existing restraining order.

If any of the above are true, this charge may result in a conviction of a Class A misdemeanor.

4.23. Misuse of 9-1-1

You commit an offense if you call or request service via text from 9-1-1 when there is no emergency. It is a crime to knowingly remain silent, abuse, or harass the 9-1-1-dispatch employee. It is also an offense to allow your phone to be used in this manner by someone else. These are all Class B misdemeanors.

Special Note: Emergency 9-1-1 systems automatically trace all calls back to a phone number and address, so it is easy to catch the caller.

4.24. Bomb Threats and False Reports to Police or Fire Departments

In addition to the 9-1-1 statute, there is a separate law that deals with bomb threats and false crime or emergency reports. You may be charged with a crime if you, knowing it to be false, report a crime in progress, like a robbery, or that someone has been injured or killed. This is a Class A misdemeanor. If the threat or false report is of an emergency involving a college or school or any public service like gas, public water, public transportation, or a power-supply facility, the charge is a State Jail felony.

4.25. Theft

This offense covers a lot of ground. It includes shoplifting; stealing street signs; stealing firewood out of someone's yard; stealing hanging plants off someone's porch; taking dairy crates, shopping carts, and items left in or around a Goodwill drop box; taking and keeping the class ring you found left in the restroom at school; or "walking" a restaurant or motel bill.

How serious the punishment is for theft depends on the value of the item taken.

Under $100—Class C misdemeanor
$100 up to $750—Class B misdemeanor
$750 up to $2,500—Class A misdemeanor
$2,500 up to $30,000—State Jail felony
$30,000 up to $150,000—Third-degree felony
$150,000 up to $300,000—Second-degree felony
$300,000 or more—First-degree felony

Very seldom will an offer to return the item or pay for it result in charges being dropped. And, if you already have a theft charge on your record, the degree of the misdemeanor or felony WILL be enhanced.

Special Note: For future employment chances, THEFT is one of the worst things to have on your record. A prospective employer is not going to believe that it was a joke or a prank. He or she will think you are dishonest, not trustworthy, and not someone he or she wants to hire.

4.26. Trespassing

If you had notice that entry was forbidden either by being told or by posted signs or the presence of an obvious enclosure intended to keep out intruders (like a fence), it is a crime to go onto the property.

If it is not a house, it is a Class B misdemeanor. Trespassing at a house or apartment is a Class A misdemeanor. Climbing the fence around the football stadium at night as a prank is a CRIME, even if you damage nothing. Climbing a TV or radio tower is also trespassing.

4.27. Evading Arrest

It is a CRIME to intentionally flee from a police officer who is attempting to arrest or detain you. This is a Class A misdemeanor, unless you flee in a car, which is a State Jail felony.

4.28. Resisting Arrest or Search

This is a Class A misdemeanor unless a deadly weapon is used—then it is a third-degree felony.

4.29. Failure to Identify

It is illegal to intentionally refuse to give your name, address, or date of birth to the officers who have lawfully arrested you. It is also illegal to give a false name, address, or date of birth, if the officer believes you to be a witness to a crime. This is a Class C misdemeanor. If you give the officer false information or refuse to give your information while being legally detained, it is a Class B. If you have a warrant already and refuse or give false info, it is a Class A misdemeanor and the charge is "Failure to Identify Fugitive."

4.30. Hindering Apprehension or Arrest

If you hide, provide aid, or warn someone that officers are seeking to arrest him or her, it is a Class A misdemeanor, unless the person you aid is charged with a felony—then your crime becomes a felony, too.

4.31. Assault

Assault comes in various categories. You have committed an assault if you intentionally or knowingly *threaten* someone with imminent bodily injury or cause physical contact that you should know is offensive, like a shove. These are Class C misdemeanors, unless committed against an elderly or disabled individual. Then the crime becomes a Class A misdemeanor.

If you intentionally and knowingly cause bodily injury to someone in an assault, it is a Class A misdemeanor, unless it is against a public servant in lawful discharge of an official duty, in which case it is a third-degree felony.

If you intentionally and knowingly assault someone causing serious bodily injury, or use a deadly weapon, this charge is a second-degree felony, unless the person assaulted is a public servant lawfully discharging his or her public duty, or the assault is in retaliation against a witness, prospective witness, or informant of a crime, then it is a first-degree felony.

An assault is defined as an unprovoked attack.

Special Note 1: In Texas, words are NEVER legal provocation for an assault. If someone refers in a negative fashion to your ancestry, you CANNOT respond by hitting that person without committing an assault. Sticks and stones may break my bones, but words may *never* hurt me.

Special Note 2: See chapter 5 Personal Relationships for information about family violence and dating violence.

4.32. Unauthorized Use of a Vehicle

Operating a car, truck, boat, or airplane without the owner's permission used to be called "joyriding." People would say they "borrowed" the vehicle with full intent to return it, rather than having stolen it with no intent to return. However, this is a State Jail felony.

4.33. Burglary of a Building

Entering a habitation or a building not then open to the public or remaining inside a building after closing hours with intent to commit a felony or theft is burglary. Burglary of a habitation (house, apartment, mobile home, etc.) is a second-degree felony. Burglary of any other building is a State Jail felony. If the burglar intends to or attempts to commit a felony other than theft, then it becomes a first-degree felony.

Special Note: Notice that this statute DOES NOT require "breaking and entering." You don't have to "break" in. If you go in through the unlocked front door, you have committed a burglary. Also, just the INTENT to commit a felony or theft is enough to convict you. You don't have to have actually committed the felony or theft just intended to.

True Story

Trey Anyone left his house on a Wednesday night to visit a friend. His friend's parents aren't home, so they open a cold one. Even though Trey is under twenty-one, he drinks enough beer to be feeling no pain. Trey and his friends leave together on foot to walk back to his house. They pass a convenience store that is obviously closed because it is dark. As they pass the rear of the store, they see the store's back door standing wide open. Someone has obviously broken in, although there is no one around.

Trey's friends have also drunk enough so that their judgment has been affected.

Instead of calling the officers or just leaving the scene, they dare Trey to go in the store to steal a candy bar. Trey accepts the dare and goes inside. A police car arrives on the scene. Trey's "friends" run away, leaving Trey in the building. He is caught inside. Trey tries to explain to the officers about the dare, but the officers arrest Trey for BURGLARY.

Trey uses his one phone call to call big brother, Steven. Steven now an expert on making bond, gets Trey out of jail. Trey hires a lawyer and hopes that the lawyer can convince the district attorney that he DID NOT burglarize the store. If he is lucky, the charge will be reduced to theft of the candy bar. The testimony of his friends will be critical.

4.34. Burglary of Coin-Operated Machines

If you break in or enter the machine in some other way, with intent to obtain money or goods, you have committed burglary of a coin-operated machine. This is a Class A misdemeanor.

4.35. Burglary of a Vehicle

Breaking into or entering into a vehicle or any part of a vehicle with intent to commit a felony or *theft* is burglary of a vehicle and punishable as a Class A misdemeanor. Notice the "enter into the vehicle" part? If you reach into an open window of a car and steal a cell phone that is on the seat of the car you have committed "Burglary of a Vehicle."

4.36. Credit or Debit Card Abuse

It is a State Jail felony to steal a credit or debit card, use or attempt to use a stolen card or a card number not your own, or to sell or buy a credit or debit card. It is also a State Jail felony to obtain property or service or attempt to obtain property or service with a fictitious credit card. It is also a State Jail felony to use a credit card knowing that it is expired, canceled, or revoked.

4.37. Forgery

If the writing you have forged is a will, codicil, deed of trust, mortgage, security instrument, security agreement, credit card, or check, it is a State Jail felony. It is a third-degree felony if the forged item is money, securities, postage, revenue stamps, or other instrument issued by a state or national government, including a driver's license or DPS-issued identification card (for further information on this, see § 2.15). Under this statute, it is illegal to possess with intent to use, to attempt to use, or to make a forged item.

4.38. False Statement to Obtain Property or Credit

It is a Class A misdemeanor to make a materially false or misleading written statement to obtain property or credit.

4.39. Tampering with Manufacturer's Identification Number

It is a Class A misdemeanor to knowingly remove, alter, or wipe out a manufacturer's permanent identification number on personal property, such as TVs, cameras, stereos, bicycles, guns, and so forth.

4.40. Rape

The main thing with rape is that either partner has the absolute RIGHT to say NO, no matter what has been said or done earlier. Provocative manner or clothing doesn't matter. It doesn't matter how many times you've done it together before. If the other partner says NO and you do it anyway, you can be charged with RAPE. It is a second-degree felony, unless a weapon, threat, or force is used, then it is a first-degree felony.

4.41. Rape Prevention

In a perfect world, you could go anywhere at any time in perfect safety. However, we must deal with reality. Just as you take precautions to prevent theft and burglary, you should take precautions to prevent rape. Your main defense is to be alert to any potential dangers and eliminate as many of them as possible. BE SMART.

4.42. What to Do If You Are Raped

If the unthinkable does happen, in spite of your immediate feelings of pain, embarrassment, humiliation, and anger, there are certain steps you must take in order to prosecute the criminal. The first step is don't make an immediate decision not to prosecute. While your feelings of wanting to forget and get on with your life and of wanting to hide what happened are natural, don't make the final decision yet. Take the following steps first. After you've taken them, you can decide later that you don't wish to prosecute, but leave the option open in the beginning.

1. Do not change clothes; straighten up the scene; shower, bathe, or douche; urinate or defecate. Any of these steps, while understandable, may destroy valuable evidence to prove you were raped.
2. Report the rape.
   a) To a rape crisis center: If your town has one, it will be listed in the phone directory. A trained volunteer will help you with police and doctor. If you do not want to report it to the police, the volunteer will not make you.
   b) To police: Even if you decide not to prosecute later, it is better to give yourself the option of prosecuting by reporting it to the police as soon as possible. Even a day's delay can mean less evidence available.
3. Get a medical exam immediately. Either through your own doctor or the emergency room, you must be examined to prove that sexual intercourse took place. Delay makes this more difficult.
4. Clothes: Don't change until told to, but be prepared to turn the clothes you were wearing over to the police. Take a change of clothes with you to the medical exam.
5. Don't suffer alone. Get help!

4.43. Should You Prosecute?

Most rapists are repeat offenders. If you do not prosecute, they may strike again, either at you or someone else. Even if you feel you don't have enough information about the rapist to prosecute, tell the police everything you know. Your information, however small, may fit in with other information and lead to the capture of the rapist. Tell the police everything you know, even if you don't want to prosecute. Some other victim may wish to do so.

City Ordinances

Before we move on, I want to share a couple of "ordinances" that seem to be quite popular across our great state. An "ordinance" is a law that is created by each city only for that city. Most cities have some form of the following two ordinances. Check with your local city secretary to see if these ordinances have been enacted in your city.

4.44. Fireworks within the City

An ordinance against possessing fireworks within the city limits. Mere *possession* of fireworks is a Class C misdemeanor.

4.45. Curfew

Some of you are not affected by a city's curfew ordinance, but you should know most cities have them. Typically, 11 p.m. on weekdays and 12 a.m. on the weekend for those of you sixteen or younger. This means that you should be inside your house after those hours; it does not mean in your yard or on your porch. Friday and Saturday night are the weekend. Daytime curfews are a big deal in larger cities. Verify if your city is one of those. Violation of a curfew ordinance is a Class C misdemeanor.

Weapons

Certain weapons are always illegal to carry or possess. Other weapons are legal to possess only in certain circumstances. Your age is very important in this section.

4.46. Illegal Weapons

It is never legal to possess, manufacture, transport, repair, or sell the following weapons:

1. An explosive weapon (bomb, grenade, rocket, or mine)
2. Machine gun or fully automatic weapon
3. Short-barrel firearm (rifle barrel shorter than sixteen inches, shotgun barrel less than eighteen inches, or overall length less than twenty-six inches)
4. Brass knuckles (including cell phone case with built-in knuckles)
5. Armor-piercing ammunition
6. A chemical dispensing device
7. A zip gun.

Except for (4) above, this offense is a third-degree felony; (4) is a Class A misdemeanors.

4.47. Legal Weapons with Restrictions

Because of your age, it is illegal to carry a handgun on your person. No one can carry on his or her person, in a public place, an illegal knife or club, although in our homes it's a different story. This is a Class A misdemeanor.

Specific Laws on Types of Weapons
1. A handgun is just what you think it is. You must be twenty-one years old to own or obtain a handgun license.
2. An illegal knife is:
   a) A knife with a blade longer than 5 1/2 inches;
   b) A hand instrument designed to cut or stab by being thrown (this appears to cover martial arts throwing stars);
   c) A dagger (including dirk, stiletto, and poniard);
   d) A bowie knife;
   e) A sword;
   f) A spear.
   Knifes and swords are being discussed currently by our state legislators. These MAY become legal to possess and or carry in late 2017.
3. A club is an instrument specially adapted or designed for the purpose of inflicting serious bodily injury or death and includes (but is not limited to):

a) A blackjack,
b) A nightstick,
c) A tomahawk,
d) Nunchuks. (If you are using them for martial arts practice, keep them in the trunk of your car when not at the dojo or your home, and you should be okay; DO NOT KEEP THEM under the seat of the car or carry them with you outside your home or place of practice. This isn't Japan, and you're not a ninja. Well, probably not a ninja.)

4.48. When You May Possess Weapons

When you are twenty-one years of age and have obtained a license to carry a handgun, you may carry a handgun on your person except where prohibited or barred by posted notice. Once twenty-one—unless you have a legal reason you can't (such as being a felon or registered gang member)—you may also possess a handgun at your home, your place of business, or *when traveling (more than across town)*. You may also possess one if you are licensed in law enforcement or if you are a private security worker or private investigator.

The section in the law on "traveling," mentioned above, is very specific. Read it. It is Texas Penal Code § 46.02. Ignorance of the law is no excuse.

4.49. Illegally Loaning Weapons

It is illegal to:

1. Loan, sell, rent, or give a gun to someone who intends to use it illegally;
2. Sell, rent, give, or offer to sell to any child under eighteen a firearm, club, illegal knife, or any martial arts throwing stars without his or her parent's permission;
3. Sell a firearm or ammunition to an intoxicated person.

These illegally loaning offenses are all Class A misdemeanors.

Drugs

This is a listing of the most commonly used drugs. Possession is without a prescription, of course.

4.50. Marijuana

Even though, in the last few years, several states in our country have decided not to prosecute anyone that possesses or smokes marijuana, IT IS *NOT* LEGAL IN TEXAS at the time of this writing. As a matter of fact, for the great majority of you, possession of it isn't allowed in those other states either. Other states have set up rules (or laws) regarding the purchase, possession, and smoking and eating of marijuana; none of these states allow people under twenty-one to do any of them.

In Texas, possession of marijuana is punished according to how much you possessed, as follows:

1. A useable amount to two ounces—Class B misdemeanor
2. More than two ounces to four ounces—Class A misdemeanor
3. More than four ounces up to five pounds—State Jail felony
4. More than five pounds up to fifty pounds—third-degree felony
5. More than fifty pounds to 2,000 pounds—second-degree felony
6. More than 2,000 pounds—five to ninety-nine years or life and a fine not to exceed $50,000.

Delivery of marijuana is punished according to how much you delivered and to whom you delivered it, as follows:

1. One-quarter ounce or less for no money—Class B misdemeanor
2. One-quarter ounce or less for money—Class A misdemeanor
3. More than 1/4 ounce but no more than five pounds—State Jail felony

4. More than five pounds but no more than fifty pounds—second-degree felony
5. More than fifty pounds but no more than 2,000 pounds—first-degree felony
6. More than 2,000 pounds—ten to ninety-nine years or life and a fine not to exceed $100,000.

Delivery of marijuana or other drugs to someone seventeen years of age or younger, or to a student enrolled in elementary or secondary school, or to someone you believe will deliver it to one of the above is a second-degree felony.

4.51. Cocaine

This includes all types and derivatives, including, but not limited to, crack and crank.

Possession:
1. Less than one gram—State Jail felony
2. One gram but less than four grams—third-degree felony
3. Four grams but less than 200 grams—second-degree felony
4. Two hundred grams but less than 400 grams—first-degree felony
5. Four hundred grams or more—ten to ninety-nine years or life and a fine not to exceed $100,000

Delivery, possession with intent to deliver, or manufacture:
1. Less than one gram—State Jail felony
2. One gram but less than four grams—second-degree felony
3. Four grams but less than 200 grams—first-degree felony
4. Two hundred grams but less than 400 grams— ten to ninety-nine years or life and a fine not to exceed $100,000
5. Four hundred grams or more—fifteen to ninety-nine years or life and a fine not to exceed $250,000

4.52. Amphetamines

Also known as speed or uppers.

Possession:

1. Less than one gram—State Jail felony
2. One gram but less than four grams—third-degree felony
3. Four grams but less than 400 grams—second-degree felony
4. Four hundred grams or more—five to ninety-nine years or life and a fine not to exceed $50,000

Delivery, manufacture, possession with intent to manufacture or deliver:

1. Less than one gram—State Jail felony
2. One gram but less than four grams—second-degree felony
3. Four grams but less than 400 grams—first-degree felony
4. Four hundred grams or more—ten to ninety-nine years or life and a fine not to exceed $100,000

4.53. Methamphetamines ("Ice" or "Ecstasy")

Same as cocaine, § 4.51.

4.54. Barbiturates

Most barbiturates, also known as downers, are treated as follows:

Possession:

1. Less than twenty-eight grams—Class A misdemeanor
2. Twenty-eight grams but less than 200 grams—third-degree felony
3. Two hundred grams but less than 400 grams—second-degree felony
4. Four hundred grams or more—five to ninety-nine years or life and a fine not to exceed $50,000.

Delivery, manufacture, or possession with intent to manufacture or deliver:

1. Less than twenty-eight grams—State Jail felony
2. Twenty-eight grams but less than 200 grams—second-degree felony

3. Two hundred grams but less than 400 grams—first-degree felony
4. Four hundred grams or more—ten to ninety-nine years or life and a fine not to exceed $100,000.

4.55. Steroids

Same as barbiturates, § 4.54.

4.56. Heroin and Morphine

Same as cocaine, § 4.51.

4.57. Drug Paraphernalia

Possession for own use: Class C misdemeanor
Possession with intent to deliver:
    First offense—Class A misdemeanor
    Second offense—ninety days to one year in jail
Sale by a person eighteen years of age or older to a person less than eighteen years of age and at least three years younger than the actor—State Jail felony.

Alcohol-Related Offenses

The consumption of alcoholic beverages plays a large role in involving many young people with the criminal justice system. Generally, it is the consumption of too much alcohol that causes problems, but some offenses concern the age of the drinker. For purposes of this section only, you are a "minor" if you are not yet twenty-one years of age.

Special Note: If you are convicted of purchase, consumption, or possession of alcoholic beverages as a minor, in addition to the punishment noted in the specific sections below, the judge must order you to attend an Alcohol-Awareness Course approved by the Texas Commission on Alcohol and Drug Abuse. Failure to attend this course within ninety days will result in suspension of your driving privileges for up to six months.

4.58. Minor in Possession (MIP)

If you are under twenty-one years of age, it is illegal to possess, consume, or purchase alcoholic beverages, unless you are in the company of your parents or your spouse who is twenty-one or older. Note that consumption (drinking it) is not required.

Frequently, the officer will issue a ticket for MIP, but he or she always has the right to arrest, if you are seventeen or older, instead.

MIP is punishable by a fine of $25 to $200 for the first offense and a fine of $500 to $1,000 for a second offense. Subsequent offenses for MIP may be enhanced to a Class B misdemeanor and filed in the county or county court-at-law. Along with the fine you will be required to attend and complete an Alcohol-Awareness Program and maybe other sanctions.

If you receive only one MIP conviction before you turn twenty-one, you can have it expunged (erased) from your criminal record by contacting the court where you were convicted. You will have to sign a sworn statement that you have received no other convictions. If you get more than one conviction, all convictions will remain on your record.

True Story

To be sure Trey doesn't get in any more trouble, Steven keeps an eye on him. Steven decides to buy some beer at a convenience store. He is twenty-one, so he can legally do so. Trey stays in the car (remember, Trey is not yet twenty-one but, man, does he like to drink). Steven puts the beer in the back seat. He does not open one, because he knows it is illegal to drink and drive.

Unbeknownst to the Anyone brothers, they are being watched by police officers. The officers decide Trey is a minor, and they stop the car. The officers ticket Trey for "Minor in Possession" (Class C misdemeanor), even though Trey is in the front seat and the beer is in the back seat. They also could have charged Steven for "Providing Alcohol to a Minor" (Class A misdemeanor).

Trey can't believe it! Back to his lawyer once again. (This lawyer could make a career out of the Anyone family!) His lawyer has a good chance of proving that Trey did not possess alcohol nor did Steven give it to him, BUT it will probably have to be done in a trial. That means substantial attorney's fees.

4.59. Providing Alcoholic Beverages to a Minor

This includes purchasing for a minor, *selling*, or giving alcohol to a minor. You can commit this offense even if you are a minor yourself. You can also be held civilly liable for damages caused by a person younger than eighteen if you provided him or her with alcohol or allowed him or her to be given alcohol while on your property (see § 4.65 below).

A parent or spouse, twenty-one or older, is the only one that can legally give alcohol to a minor. That does not mean your best friend's parent, even if he or she is *like-a-parent* to you. Only your parent.

All three, purchasing, selling, or providing alcohol to a minor, are Class A misdemeanors, with a fine up to $4,000 and/or confinement in jail for up to one year. Your driver's license or ability to get one will be automatically suspended for 180 days if there is a conviction.

4.60. Misrepresentation of Age by a Minor

If you say you are twenty-one or older, the punishment is $25 to $200 for the first offense and $100 to $500 for subsequent offenses. Sanctions will apply on this charge as well.

4.61. Public Intoxication

A person in a public place—regardless of age—who is intoxicated to the degree that he or she is a danger to himself or herself or others, violates the law.

No sobriety tests are required. The officer's opinion is all that is necessary for an arrest. This offense is a Class C misdemeanor. In rare instances, the officer, at his or her discretion, may choose to write you a citation and release you to a parent or guardian, rather than arrest you. Intoxication is not only from alcohol. A person may be charged with Public Intoxication if they are intoxicated by drugs, prescription or not, as well. The most important words in the law on this are: "he or she is intoxicated to the level that he or she is a danger to himself, herself or others."

4.62. Signs of Intoxication

There are many signs of intoxication. You may exhibit many or few of those I will list. Remember, an officer must only know that you are intoxicated and believe you to be a danger to yourself or to others for you to be charged with an offense.

Coordination:
    Stands with feet wide apart for balance
    Leans against structure for support
    Fumbles with wallet or money
    Slurs or trips over words while speaking
Reduced judgment and inhibitions:
    Becomes overly excited
    Speaks loudly and or profanely
    Throws objects
    Giggles or laughs for no apparent reason
Reflexes:
    Slow or deliberate movements
    Slow or no response to questions
    Slow or no reaction to actions such as spilling beer on
     oneself
Vision:
    Red or watery eyes
    Droopy eyelids or tired appearance
    Squints continuously
    Closes or covers one eye to remove double vision

Appearance:
    Frequently rubs hands through hair or on face
    Sometimes has involuntary eye movement
    Frequent trips to the bathroom

4.63. Open-Container Law

It is illegal to drink and drive or for a passenger to have any type of open container (any open alcoholic beverage) within a vehicle. This is a Class C misdemeanor.

4.64. Alcoholic Beverages at Public Schools

Possession of any alcoholic beverage on public school grounds, in public school buildings, or at public school athletic stadiums is a Class C misdemeanor.

This DOES NOT apply to state universities and colleges. Each university or college's governing board adopts rules controlling possession and sale of alcoholic beverages on its campus. The rules vary from campus to campus.

4.65. If You Are the Party Host Serving Alcoholic Beverages

In addition to the criminal penalty for providing alcoholic beverages to a minor in § 4.59, you may, as a private party host or as an officer or member of an organization that is hosting a party where YOU or YOUR ORGANIZATION provides alcohol, have additional responsibilities. In *many states*, a private party host or officers and members of an organization hosting a party have a legal duty NOT TO SERVE an intoxicated person regardless of age. If an intoxicated person leaves the party and has an accident, the private hosts or officers and members of the organization are legally responsible to pay money for any damages incurred. It is only smart to protect yourself against a possible lawsuit, by CONTROLLING THE AMOUNT OF ALCOHOL SERVED. Don't let a friend drive home drunk. You may not only be saving his or her life and someone else's, but you may also be saving yourself a lawsuit.

Texas DOES have a law that makes anyone who SELLS ALCOHOLIC BEVERAGES legally responsible if he or she sells to an intoxicated person and there is an accident.

4.66. Driving Under the Influence by a Minor (DUI)

It is a violation of the law if a minor operates a motor vehicle or a watercraft, in a public place, with *any detectable amount* of alcohol in the minor's system. "Any detectable amount" is not defined in the law, but you should know if you have been drinking, usually an officer can smell it. You don't have to be intoxicated (see DWI below) to be charged with DUI . . . because we all know at your age; you can't legally drink *any* alcohol. DUI is a Class C misdemeanor, and anyone convicted must complete specific sanctions along with paying the fine. If it is a first offense, the fine is not more than $500 but you must complete twenty to forty hours of community service also. If you have been convicted before for DUI, the number of community service hours will be increased and the fine can go up to as much as $2,000.

Special Note: Above where I mentioned that officers can smell the alcohol on you, that works for weed too. If you smoke in your car spraying perfume as the officer walks up doesn't work.

4.67. Driving While Intoxicated (DWI)

It is illegal to drive a motor vehicle in a public place if intoxicated.

Intoxicated means:
1. Not having the normal use of mental or physical faculties by reason of the consumption of alcohol, a controlled substance, a drug, or a combination of two or more such substances;
2. Having an alcohol concentration in your blood of .08 percent or more.

If stopped by the police, you will be questioned and you may be given a roadside sobriety test (this is not required). If the officer decides you are intoxicated, you will be offered a breath test. If you refuse to take the breath test or give a blood sample, a blood warrant will be requested by the officer. Once a blood warrant is received from a magistrate, more than likely you will be transported and your blood collected. Your driver's license will be suspended for ninety days with no probation if you are twenty-one or older. If you are under twenty-one, the suspension is for at least one year. If you go to trial, the fact that you refused can be told to the judge or jury. You do not have a right to talk to your attorney BEFORE taking the test. If you take the breath test and score .08 or higher, your license will be suspended for at least sixty days, regardless of whether you are prosecuted for DWI or not.

At the jail or police station, you will probably be video recorded, especially if you refuse the breath test. This video can be shown at your trial.

Special Note: Know the difference. In Texas, Driving Under the Influence (DUI) is driving with any "detectable" amount. Driving While Intoxicated (DWI) is not having the normal use of mental or physical faculties.

The punishment for DWI is as follows:

1. Class B misdemeanor with confinement in jail for not less than seventy-two hours.
2. If previously convicted of DWI one time (including probation), it is a Class A misdemeanor with confinement in jail for at least thirty days. You will most likely also be required to place a Breath Analysis Machine on your vehicle. This machine will cost you to have installed and will not allow the vehicle to be started if ethyl alcohol is detected in the breath of the vehicle's operator.
3. If previously convicted two or more times, it is a third-degree felony. Same thing as above with the Breath Analysis Machine.

If there was serious bodily injury to someone else, a death, or an open container of alcohol in the car, the fines and jail time increase. You will also have your driver's license suspended for 90 to 365 days on the first conviction of DWI. This is a separate suspension from refusal to take the breath test, or scoring .08 or higher on the breath test.

Your insurance premiums will increase.

Special Note: Flying a plane or piloting a boat while intoxicated is treated the same as DWI.

4.68. Intoxication Assault

If you cause serious bodily injury to another while driving, flying, or boating while intoxicated, it is a third-degree felony.

4.69. Intoxication Manslaughter

If you cause the death of another while driving, flying, or boating while intoxicated, it is a second-degree felony.

4.70. Texas Penal Code § 19.02 Murder

You may also be charged with murder, if while committing a felony, you perform an act "clearly dangerous to human life that causes the death of an individual." A third DWI conviction is a felony offense. This means that if your act of driving while intoxicated results in a person's death, and you have two previous DWI convictions, you can be charged with MURDER.

4.71. Texas Alcoholic Beverage Commission (TABC)

If you would like to get in touch with the commission or receive more information on alcohol and its effects, please do.

Texas Alcoholic Beverage Commission
www.tabc.texas.gov
www.2young2drink.com
PO Box 13127
Austin, Texas 78711
(512) 206-3420
(1-888) THE-TABC
[(1-888) 843-8222]

Chapter 5

PERSONAL RELATIONSHIPS

Yep, we have to talk about it because there are some specific laws regarding our personal relationships. The following few pages will explain everything from dating violence charges to sexting laws to marriage and divorce.

You may already be in an intimate relationship—and it may be great right now—but all relationships are tough, especially for young people. These days it seems they may be getting even tougher with the rate of dating violence charges increasing the way it is.

Assault charges were discussed in the "Specific Crimes" section of chapter 4, but we need to add another couple of layers to that subject. We will do that here with an explanation of "family violence" and "dating violence," which are both forms of assault. Family violence is typically an assault that concerns a family member related by blood or marriage, as well as anyone living together in the same household. It also means anyone who once lived together but does not now. A wife or ex-wife, husband or ex-husband, child, parent, roommate, or ex-roommate are good examples.

5.1. Dating Violence

Dating violence typically relates to relationship abuse and is defined as a pattern of violent behavior that one uses against a past or present girlfriend or boyfriend. A Center for Disease Control study has found that *nearly 1.5 million high school students nationwide experience physical abuse from a dating partner every year*. However, please realize that abuse isn't always physical. That same study tells us that *one in three young people in the United States is a victim of physical as well as sexual, emotional, or verbal abuse from a dating partner*. This behavior is usually brought on by the abuser's desire to establish power, control, and dominance over a partner and may be done through intimidation and fear. Keep in mind this type of violence does not require those involved to be in a long-term, committed relationship but can occur in casual relationships as well. If in a casual relationship (coworker, friend, classmate), it is typically filed as a criminal assault charge, as discussed in chapter 4, not as family violence or dating violence.

As a victim of dating violence, you have the option of seeking both criminal and civil remedies against the assaultive person. Criminal assault charges may be filed against the alleged offender and can range from misdemeanor to felony charges, depending on the circumstances.

The charges and potential penalties depend on the degree of harm or threat and other factors, such as previous violence convictions in a court.

Family/dating violence or assault is:

- Class C misdemeanor if the victim suffered no physical pain or lasting harm. This could include even a threat of violence.
- Class A misdemeanor if the contact caused pain (like a slap), left a physical mark (cut or bruise), or resulted in lasting injury (such as a broken jaw).
- Third-degree felony for strangulation (choking) or if the abuser has prior domestic violence convictions. (See ranges of punishment under "Specific Crimes" in chapter 4.)

In addition to jail time and a criminal record, a person may receive other lasting consequences if convicted of family/dating violence or family/dating assault, such as:

- Not being able to own or possess a firearm.
- Not being able to get a Texas hunting or fishing license.
- A person's current or future employment may be affected, especially pilots, military personnel, teachers, health care workers, and city, county, or state employees.
- It could affect a divorce or child custody arrangement.

Special Note: Dating violence may also be charged if the victim of an assault is the boyfriend, girlfriend, husband or wife of the assaultive person's ex (Texas Family Code § 71.0021).

Protective Orders

As a victim of an assault or family/dating violence, you may also choose to file for a protective order. This order is granted to give victims protection from the assaultive person and future acts of assault and/or stalking.

The protective order may include other rules the individual must follow. Things like how far he or she must stay from the victim and the victim's household, work, or school. Most protective orders require that the abusive person not make any contact at all, even through phone calls or text, to the victim or the victim's family members. The abuser may be ordered to attend counseling or other special classes. A protective order is only issued by a judge and is generally in place up to two years.

Some victims consider a protective order to be ineffective when dealing with family or dating violence. Protective orders are only paper and do not offer twenty-four-hour police protection. Keep in mind it is explained to the abuser by the judge that, if found to be in violation of the order, the abuser will be arrested and may be forced to pay fines or even serve jail time. A protective order may not protect a person from someone who doesn't think about consequences or care about being arrested.

You may file for a protective order through your local district clerk's office.

A protective order is often confused with a restraining order. . . . Don't do that! (see § 5.24 Restraining Orders).

5.2. Send Nudes!

No! Please don't! The reality every young person should know is that it is possible for you to be charged with a crime for sexting. It is a misdemeanor or a felony offense for possession or promotion of child pornography, depending on the circumstances. Sexting has become very popular with young people in the last several years with many of your generation seeing this as an ordinary part of life. If you are unaware, sexting refers to sending nude or sexually explicit photos or messages with your cell phone. Most of the time, the person in the photos either agrees to the photo being taken or takes the picture and sends it to a boyfriend/girlfriend or someone he or she is attracted to. The hope of the sender, in most cases, is for the picture to be kept private by the person that received it. More and more of these photos are being posted on the internet through social-media apps, or shared with others through text or email though. In many cases, "sharing" is done without the knowledge of the person in the photo. I know, you only sent it because you wanted to get his or her attention or to be funny, but there is a good chance it could have a very negative effect on your reputation or relationships with friends or family. You open yourself up to being cyberbullied; in addition, your participation in activities at school, getting into college, or even getting the job you want could all be on the line.

Special Note: The MTV News special "Sexting in America: When Privates go Public" states that nearly one in five sexting recipients (17 percent) report that they have passed the images along to someone else, with more than half saying that they just assumed others would want to see them (52 percent). Others expressed a desire to show off (35 percent), and others were motivated by boredom (26 percent).

5.3. Sexting Penalties

The penalties for this crime can vary considerably based on who is involved in the case. Typically, the penalty for minors who are convicted of sending sexually explicit messages or photos to another minor will be less severe than for adults (those eighteen years of age or older).

For example, the penalties for a minor on a first-time sexting conviction could include:

- Conviction of a Class C misdemeanor with a fine of up to $500;
- And/or mandatory participation in an educational program about the dangers of sexting.

If a minor sends the sexually explicit material to someone, who they know will feel harassed, annoyed, alarmed, abused, tormented, embarrassed, or offended the charge may be filed as a Class B misdemeanor (up to 180 days in jail, fine up to $2,000, or both).

It may be filed as a Class A misdemeanor (up to one year in jail, fine up to $4,000, or both) if a minor has been previously convicted of *promoting (sending) the visual material with intent to harass, annoy, alarm, abuse, torment, embarrass, or offend* someone.

Those eighteen or older who engage in sharing sexually explicit photos *with minors* are subject to much greater penalties. The law does not take into account that you are still a senior in high school. That birthday is so important! Adults may face child pornography charges, possibly leading to:

- Conviction of a third-degree felony;
- Incarceration in prison for two to ten years;
- A fine up to $10,000;
- And/or registration as a sex offender (for life).

If an adult, eighteen or older, receives sexually explicit messages *from a minor* and then attempts to send or share the message with other adults, the charge could be enhanced (or upgraded) to intent to distribute child pornography. This type of charge could lead to:

- Conviction of a second-degree felony;
- Incarceration in prison for two to twenty years;
- A fine of up to $10,000;
- And/or registration as a sex offender (for life)

Special Note: All three of the above examples are related to sharing sexually explicit photos of minors under the age of eighteen. If the minor involved is under fourteen years of age, the case may be enhanced to an even higher charge.

5.4. Protections from Prosecution for Minors

As stated above, the punishments in Texas for those under the age of eighteen are not nearly as strict because certain legal provisions may offer protection for those accused in some sexting cases. These protections have been put in the law to protect the reputation of minors and allow them to learn from their mistakes. If a minor meets certain conditions, he or she may be exempt from being prosecuted in court. To qualify for the protections, the conditions the minors must meet in a sexting case are:

- Sender and receiver are no more than two years apart in age;
- Sender and receiver must both be minors;
- Photos are only exchanged between the sender and receiver;
- Photos are exchanged only in the context of a dating relationship;
- Sender has never been convicted of sending sexually explicit photos before;
- And the receiver destroyed the visual material within a reasonable amount of time;
- Or was married to the sender at the time of the offense.

Anything sent through the internet becomes virtually impossible to control and has the potential to be shared with a worldwide audience. You and your boyfriend or girlfriend may love and trust each other . . . but remember relationships are tough and couples break up.

True Story

It is Saturday night, and Trey has had a rough couple of weeks and feels he needs to blow off a little steam. He knows Caleb and Aaron Pushover's mom is out of town, so it doesn't take much to talk them into having a party. It will be great! They live in the country, so Trey's girlfriend Kayla Bae can tell her dad she is staying with a friend, meet him there, and spend the night. Trey knows it is the perfect plan. Sixteen-year-olds don't get this type of freedom very often. He will have a few drinks, relax with friends, and have that special time with Kayla. No driving, no cops, no trouble.

Not two minutes before he gets to Caleb and Aaron's house, he gets a text from Kayla. She can't come ☹. Dad has figured this one out and knows Momma Pushover is out of town. No deal! Even though he is upset she tried to pull this off, he says Trey can come to their house. Trey knows how her dad is though. He's staying at the party.

Now Kayla is mad at Trey. She knows Malorie, his ex, will be there, and Malorie still has a thing for him and she hates Kayla.

Kayla wants to remind Trey what he is missing, so she sends a few sexy pictures.

Trey has had just enough beer that he is turned on but has learned how drinking and driving turns out. C'mon, he's Steven's brother, and they don't have the best luck behind the wheel.

Trey decides the only thing to do is stay put and get drunk.

The pictures keep coming and getting sexier. Trey can't handle it anymore, and he has to share his great fortune with those less fortunate. He tells Matt and Michael to sit beside him and have their minds blown. As they hoot and holler and stare at the screen, Malorie wants to see too. "No way," Trey screams. "This is guy stuff."

A couple hours later, Trey is passed out on the couch with his phone on his chest, and Malorie can't stand not knowing what was so amazing. She takes his phone, uses his thumb to unlock it, and there they are. Pictures of Kayla in all her glory!

"Watch this!" she thinks as she sends them to herself then to everyone in her Snapchat list. "Now everyone will know what type of girl Kayla is." She whispers to herself as she hits the little blue arrow.

Of course, we all know what happens here. Screenshots are taken, the police do get involved, and multiple lives are thrown into turmoil. Trey is charged with a Class C misdemeanor for showing his sixteen-year-old buddies. He loses Kayla but claims in court a protection for minors. He gets off with only having to attend some classes. Malorie gets it bad though. Some of the recipients of her snap are high school seniors and are already eighteen. Plus, she sent it to embarrass Kayla and that goal was achieved. Kayla is humiliated and ridiculed for years to come, but Malorie has to hire her own attorney to go to court to defend her actions on a Class B misdemeanor harassment charge. Nobody won on this one.

Gifts

5.5. Gifts between Dating Couples

If you are dating someone and give that person various gifts, you do NOT have a legal right to demand a return of those gifts when you break up.

Living Together

If you live together openly and never tell people that you are married, then no common-law marriage (§ 5.17) exists, regardless of how long you live together. Children are not automatically legitimate but can be legitimated through the courts. Property purchased together is jointly owned. There is no legal process necessary to end this relationship. This makes it easy to walk away, BUT if there are children or you cannot agree on a property division, the end can be messy. If the parents of children split without agreeing about support, it may be necessary to go to court for a support order or to prove paternity (who the father is). A court action can be used to divide any jointly purchased property. Anything bought solely with your own salary is your separate property to keep.

Because of all the potential problems, think long and hard before you live together as a long-term relationship.

If you want to stay out of court, DO NOT COMMINGLE YOUR FUNDS.

Paternity

5.6. Guys

If you father a child, you have responsibilities to that child that can be enforced in court, if necessary, even if you never marry the mother.

1. Before the child is born: As the father, you have no legal rights before the child is born. You have no right to demand an abortion or prevent one. You have no control over whether the mother smokes, drinks, or has adequate medical care. You also have no legal duty to provide money for medical expenses. However, after the child is born, if you are named the father by the court, you can be ordered to pay half of the birth medical expenses along with child support.
2. After the child is born:
   a) If the mother keeps the child:
      (1) If you admit that you are the father, you are agreeing to take on the responsibility of child support until that child is eighteen. It is a good idea to do this through a court

paternity proceeding so that the amounts are spelled out, and if you desire, you may have visitation rights.

(2) If you do not admit that the child is yours, the child's mother can file a PATERNITY suit against you to try to prove that you are the father. This is done through testimony (yours, hers, and any other witnesses) and blood tests. Blood tests can be ordered by the court, if necessary. If found YOU ARE THE FATHER, you can be ordered to pay support until the child is eighteen and be granted visitation rights. You can be sued for paternity any time until the child reaches age twenty.

(3) The mother can ask you to give up all rights and responsibilities to the child by signing a "waiver of interest." You give up your rights FOREVER and have no duty to pay support, but you also lose any visitation rights to the child.

b) If the mother puts the child up for adoption:

(1) If you don't want the child yourself, you will be asked to sign the "waiver of interest" or an "affidavit of relinquishment" giving up your rights FOREVER. You'll have no contact with the child and no duty to support the child.

(2) If you DO want the child, you must hire a lawyer and intervene in the adoption proceeding. If you admit to being the father and the mother admits it, you have a better chance to get the child than strangers would.

Child Support—Both Mom and Dad

5.7. Child-Support Amounts

As the parent of a child, you *must* provide support for that child until the child is eighteen, or longer if the child is disabled. This section applies to both mom and dad.

The noncustodial parent (the parent that does not have full or majority custody) will be ordered by the court to pay a specific amount of support, usually monthly, whether the child is legitimate or not. The minimum amounts of support are set by law as follows:

1. One child: 20 percent of net income
2. Two children: 25 percent of net income
3. Three children: 30 percent of net income
4. Four children: 35 percent of net income
5. Five children: 40 percent of net income
6. Six or more: not less than the amount for five children.

Net income means gross pay minus income tax withholding, social security (F.I.C.A.), and insurance coverage for the child, if so ordered. You can agree with the other parent on a different amount of child support.

5.8. Child Visitation

The parents may reach their own agreement, but if they do not, the law sets the visitation for the noncustodial parent. The statute provides specific times if the parents live less than one hundred miles apart or more than one hundred miles apart. Since the statute goes into great detail, it is beyond the scope of this book. If you wish to read the statute, go to the reference section of the public library and ask for the Texas statutes. Look in the second volume of the Texas Family Code at §§ 153.312 and 153.313 or look these up online.

Marriage

GETTING THE MARRIAGE LICENSE

5.9. Both Must Go

Go to your county clerk's office with your future spouse. Both of you must go in person, and they will give you a formal application. You must be at least sixteen, but if you are under the age of eighteen, you will need a certified copy of your birth certificate and judicial approval or parental consent.

5.10. The Oath

You will both have to take an oath that is printed on the application and sign it in front of the clerk. Keep in mind, you don't have to get married in the county you get your license, but your license is only good for a marriage ceremony within Texas.

5.11. Identification

You will have to prove your identity and age. You can do this with a driver's license or and ID. This identification can NOT be torn, damaged, or expired. You may also use a passport or a valid government or military ID.

5.12. Pay the fee

The fee is generally seventy to eighty-five dollars depending on where you get your license. If you take the State of Texas–approved marriage education class as a couple, sixty dollars will be waived from the price.

5.13. Set the Date

You must have the ceremony within ninety days after the marriage license was issued. You must also wait seventy-two hours (three days) after obtaining the license to have your ceremony. There is an exception to this rule for active military personnel.

5.14. Who will Perform the Ceremony?

In our state, you must have a ceremony, so you will need to find someone to perform that ceremony, and it can only be performed by specific people. Those who qualify: a licensed or ordained Christian minister or priest, a Jewish rabbi, or a person who is an officer in a religious organization authorized by that organization to conduct the marriage ceremony.

Others qualified to marry people in Texas are a judge of a municipal court; a judge or magistrate of a federal court of Texas; a justice of the court of appeals or supreme court; judge of the criminal appeals court; judge of the district, county, or probate courts; judge of the county courts-at-law; judge of the courts of domestic relations; judge of juvenile courts; and retired justice or judge of those courts; or a current or retired justice of the peace.

5.15. Everyone Must Attend

Seems obvious, but, yes, you must both be at the ceremony to get married. The only exception is if you or your future spouse is a member of the United States military who is stationed in another country in combat or another military operation.

5.16. What Happens to the Marriage License?

When the ceremony concludes, the person who conducted the marriage should record the date and county where the ceremony was performed, and he or she (or you) will return it to the county clerk where you got it. It must be turned in within thirty days of the ceremony.

Realize, a wedding can cost as little as forty bucks but a divorce is usually about $3,000.

Special Note: A United States Supreme Court ruling in the case of Obergefell vs. Hodges on June 26, 2015, made it possible for same-sex partners to follow the exact steps above and have a legally binding wedding ceremony and marriage.

5.17. Common-Law Marriage

A common-law marriage is a marriage that has had no official wedding ceremony. Children born are legitimate. Property acquired during the marriage is community property under most circumstances. To end a common-law marriage, you must file for divorce.

How do you create a common-law marriage? By living together for a reasonable period of time, holding yourself out to others as being married.

What is a "reasonable" period of time? There is no magic answer. Probably two weeks is enough; probably two days is not enough. The time in between is in limbo. In other words, it is up to the courts. The judge or jury could find two or three days as a reasonable time or not, depending on the individual circumstances.

What is "holding yourself out to others as being married"? This means that one of you uses the other's last name maybe or you introduce each other as husband or wife. You could sign your lease or seek credit as a married couple. In other words, if you act like you are married or say you are married . . . you are married.

What if you tell only your landlord that you are married, because you know that he or she will not rent to you otherwise, but to your friends you say you are just living together? Probably you don't have a common-law marriage, but the more places you put your names as a married couple, the more likely you are to create a common-law marriage.

What if you have filed for dependent status with the US Armed Forces or have filed a joint tax return with the IRS? You have a common-law marriage.

Special Note: If the common-law marriage comes to an end, you should file for divorce within one year.

5.18. Community Property

Texas is a community property state. Any salary you earn is community property if you are married at the time you earn it. It belongs half to you and half to your spouse. Anything you purchase with that salary becomes community property. Any other income you receive while you are married, such as interest on a savings account, is also community property, even if the savings account itself is your separate property. In fact, there are only two common ways to obtain separate property while you are married, as a gift or as an inheritance.

You can agree to keep income as separate property, if you sign a prenuptial agreement before you marry. You need an attorney to prepare this document for you.

Upon divorce, community property is divided by the spouses, or if no agreement can be reached, by the judge or jury. Generally speaking, each party is entitled to half of the assets.

Debts are also treated as community property if incurred while married, unless only one spouse's separate property was used as collateral. This is a lengthy subject with many possible variations. If you are involved in a divorce with disputes over property or debts, you may be better off to HIRE A LAWYER.

5.19. Separate Property

Any property you own before marriage remains separate property after marriage, as long as you can trace it. If you confuse it with community by mingling the two together, you may not be able to claim it as separate property later in a divorce. Inheritances and gifts made solely to you are also separate property, even if made after marriage.

5.20. Wedding Gifts

Generally speaking, wedding gifts given to both of you are treated as community property. They belong half to each spouse, regardless of whose relative gave the gift. The court will divide them equally if you do not reach your own agreement.

If a wedding gift, such as lingerie, was given to one particular spouse, then it is that spouse's separate property.

5.21. Engagement Rings

In almost all cases, if the wedding is called off, any ring must be given back to the giver. This is because an engagement ring is a conditional gift, not an absolute gift. It is conditional on the marriage taking place. If the giver does not want the ring back, it does not have to be returned.

5.22. Legal Separation

There is no such thing as legal separation in Texas. You are either married or divorced. You must separate to file for divorce and live apart for sixty days during the time the divorce is pending, but this "separation" is not a legal status.

Some states have three separate categories—married, legal separation by court decree, and divorce. Texas does not.

5.23. Divorce

This is a complicated and lengthy subject, beyond the scope of this book, but I will give you some basic information.

1. Grounds (reasons) for divorce: Texas has a no-fault divorce system that only requires that one party wants out. This party must be willing to swear to incompatibility (can't get along) under oath in court. The old grounds of adultery, cruelty, abandonment, and so forth, are still on the books but seldom used. There is no reason to use these "fault" grounds. Generally, the court's job in a divorce is NOT TO PUNISH THE OTHER PARTY but to end the marriage. If you insist on filing the divorce under one of the "fault" grounds, you will find your attorney's fees are extremely expensive.

2. One attorney cannot represent both parties: an attorney can represent only one spouse, even if the other spouse is not contesting the divorce and doesn't hire an attorney.

3. Must you hire an attorney to get a divorce? No, if you have no kids and no property. Several "how-to" books are available at bookstores. The books are inexpensive and provide the forms needed with instructions. If you have kids or property, it's possible but may be a little more difficult without an attorney.

4. Alimony (spousal support): There is temporary support during the time the divorce is pending and permanent support for up to three years, if the marriage lasted at least ten years and the spouse is not able to be self-supporting. You

must hire a lawyer to get alimony, and it is granted only in certain instances.

5. How long does it take? The divorce petition must be on file for sixty days before a final hearing can be held. It may take longer than that for various reasons.

5.24. Restraining Order

A restraining order is much like a protective order (discussed above) but is only used when civil cases have been filed, meaning a restraining order preserves property and protects people when a lawsuit has been filed, including when someone files for divorce, child custody, or to change a child custody court order.

A restraining order orders someone NOT to do certain things, such as:

- Not to harm your property;
- Not to harass, threaten, or harm you or your children;
- Not to remove a spouse from the common home;
- Not to spend great sums of money until divorce proceedings are settled;
- Or a restraining order may be used as a temporary order for child custody.

There are three different types of restraining orders. These three are:

- Temporary restraining order—lasts up to fourteen days;
- Temporary injunction—lasts until the day of the final order of the court where the lawsuit has been filed;
- Permanent injunction—lasts until another order is filed by the court where the lawsuit has been filed.

If a restraining order is broken or violated by the person it has been placed on, the police, most of the time, will not arrest if you call them. They may stop the violator from doing what he or she is doing but not the violation. The violation may result in new criminal charges for the violator, but the violation itself, like being within so many feet of the victim for example, will need to be handled in the court with jurisdiction of the lawsuit.

You may file a restraining order when you file paperwork for a lawsuit or after as long as the paperwork is filed in the same court as the lawsuit.

5.25. Annulment

This is dissolution of a marriage as though it never existed. The process is very similar to divorce and costs the same or more. Annulment is only allowed in the following special circumstances:

1. Underage, or less than eighteen years old when married without a parent's permission, IF filed within ninety days of the marriage, as long as the minor has not turned eighteen;
2. Marriage under the influence of alcohol or drugs;
3. Impotency (look it up);
4. Marriage through fraud, duress, or force;
5. Mental incompetency;
6. Concealed divorce;
7. Marrying a close relative.

True Story

"What can I do for you?" the lawyer asks.

"I want a divorce or annulment or out somehow. It was all a terrible mistake. Teri Ladylove and I ran off and got married, even though our parents didn't want us to. Now, I can see that they were right," says Steven Anyone.

"How long have you been married?" the lawyer asks.

"One week," Steven replies.

"One week! Don't you think you're being a little hasty? Lots of people need a little while to adjust to each other."

"No, I know it isn't going to work. I want out as painlessly and cheaply as possible," says Steven.

"Are you both eighteen?" asks the lawyer.

"Yes."

"Then you will probably have to have a divorce, not an annulment. It is a lot easier and cheaper to get into marriage than it is to get out of it. I can file the papers quite soon, but the law requires that the final hearing can't be held until the sixty-first day after filing," says the lawyer.

"Whatever you say. My mind is made up. I want out," says Steven. "What will it cost?"

Once more, acting hastily has gotten Steven in trouble. Once more, he is making his lawyer richer.

Chapter 6

___

EMPLOYMENT AND CONSUMER CONCERNS AND OTHER ISSUES

This chapter contains brief legal information on a variety of topics.

Employment

6.1. Getting Fired

Under Texas law, you can be fired for no reason. There is no requirement that you be warned first or that you have done anything wrong. Also, severance pay is not required.

This rule has some exceptions.

1. Contract: If you are employed under a union contract or another written agreement, your contract probably sets forth the way you can be fired. Read it and find out. If it doesn't, then you can be fired as stated above.
2. Company policy: All government agencies (municipal, county, state, or federal) and some private businesses have written procedures for firing. Generally, you can

only be fired for doing something wrong, and frequently you must be warned first. Businesses are not required to have such a procedure, but if the business has imposed on itself a procedure, then it must be followed. Usually, this procedure is set forth in an employee handbook or policy statement. If you don't have a handbook, ask your personnel office for one. If there is no handbook, there is usually no procedure.

Special Note: You cannot legally be fired for refusing to break the law if your boss orders you to do something illegal. However, he or she can wait and fire you later for no cause.

6.2. Discrimination

It is illegal to fire, refuse to promote, or refuse to hire based on race, religion, sex, or color. Problems of discrimination in employment can be reported to the human or civil rights commission through the Texas Workforce Commission:

Texas Workforce Commission
101 E. 15th Street
Austin, Texas 78778-0001
(512) 463-2222
http://www.twc.state.tx.us/partners/civil-rights-discrimination.

This complaint needs to be in writing. You can also complain to the Federal Equal Employment Opportunity Commission (EEOC) at the following addresses:

EEOC Headquarters
US Equal Employment Opportunity Commission
131 M Street, NE
Washington, DC 20507
(202)663-4900
Or

Dallas District Office
207 South Houston Street
3rd Floor
Dallas, TX 75202

El Paso Area Office
300 E. Main Drive
Suite 500
El Paso, TX 79901

Houston District Office
Mickey Leland Building
1919 Smith Street
6th Floor
Houston, TX 77002

San Antonio Field Office
Legacy Oaks, Building A
5410 Fredericksburg Road
Suite 200
San Antonio, TX 78229

The phone number for all EEOC offices in our state is the same. (1-800) 669-4000. The operator will transfer you to your closest office. The EEOC website is https://www.eeoc.gov/.

Complaints to these agencies are free. You may also have grounds for a private civil lawsuit. If so, you must find your own attorney for this. Most attorneys will take this kind of case on a contingent-fee basis—that is, they receive their pay from your winnings, if any. You have to pay filing costs, win or lose. Remember, lawsuits can win big bucks but can take a long time.

Special Note: Discrimination on the basis of age or handicap is permitted in some situations if done on reasonable grounds. Complaints in these two areas should be made to the same agencies noted above.

6.3. Sexual Harassment

It is illegal to sexually harass an employee. What constitutes sexual harassment? Certainly, requiring sexual favors for promotion or to retain a job is clearly sexual harassment. Other things include inappropriate language, touching, and an atmosphere that intimidates a worker. The only way to stop such harassment is to COMPLAIN to the highest-ranking supervisor possible. If the employer fails to correct the situation, you can complain to the Equal Employment Opportunity Commission at the addresses given above. If all else fails, or if you are not satisfied with the results, you may hire your own lawyer and file a civil lawsuit. A lawyer may be willing to represent you on a contingent-fee basis—that is, no fee from you unless you win your lawsuit.

Consumer Credit

The state of your credit can be of prime importance to you in our society. It can affect not only your ability to obtain a loan or a new credit card but also your ability to rent an apartment or even get a job.

For the remainder of this chapter, we will discuss your credit history, the collection of debts, and what rights you have if you are being contacted by a debt collector.

6.4. Credit-Reporting Agency

This is a private company that records your credit both good and bad. The agency is supported by merchants who pay to be members and who pay to get credit reports. Besides listing bad things like court judgments, past-due accounts, and late payments, good credit is listed too.

Bad things stay on your credit history for seven years. If you file bankruptcy, it will stay on your credit history for ten years.

Some lenders or credit card companies will give you new credit, even if you have some bad credit, but most will not.

You can view or get a copy of your credit history online for free or by paying a small fee. (Do NOT give the credit history website your credit/debit card number. If it is a free service, why would they need your credit/debit card number?) If you have been denied credit because of something bad on your credit history, you can ask to see your credit history for free from the company that denied you, if you do so within thirty days of the denial.

6.5. Before Your Debt Goes to a Collection Agency

It is much easier to make a deal with the creditor you owe money to than a collection agency. Explain in writing what you can afford to pay monthly, and enclose the first payment (not cash) to show good faith. Include a description of how much money you make each month and what your other debts are. The creditor is far more likely to accept your monthly payments if he or she can see that there is no way you can pay more. Don't put in writing anything that you don't intend to do. Don't skip payments. Even if the creditor refuses this arrangement over the phone, try it in writing. You have nothing to lose, and sometimes the creditor will accept.

Do not expect a creditor (someone or business that has in the past given you credit) to give you any special consideration because you quit your full-time job to go to school. That was your decision, and when you made it, you knew that you owed money.

Do all of the following before a collection agency is involved. Once one is involved, you must deal only with the collection agency. The creditor will not intervene.

Collection agencies are much less likely to accept a monthly installment agreement for small amounts of money. They will want all of the amount owed at once or in large installments. Sometimes they will offer to settle for less than the full amount of debt owed if paid all at once.

6.6. Collection Agency

Do not confuse a collection agency with a credit-reporting agency. A collection agency is a private company which may be hired by a creditor to collect money from you. Sometimes a single company may be both a collection agency and a credit-reporting agency.

Collection agencies will contact you by phone and by mail, repeatedly if necessary, to try to get you to pay what you owe. There are laws regulating what kind of contact is allowed. They will be discussed in following sections.

Once the debt is at the collection agency, you must deal with the agency. It is usually too late to make a deal with the merchant (the person or company you owe money to, or that has extended you credit).

Do not let a collector keep you on the phone wasting both your time and his or hers. If you can't pay, say so and politely hang up. Realize, this is not the end of it though. For further information on what collectors can and can't do, see the following sections.

If unable to collect from you, the next step is suit in court.

Special Note: The following rules apply to the collection agency, not necessarily to the creditor. The creditor may or may not have to follow the same rules. If in doubt about the actions of a creditor, contact the Texas Attorney General's Office for Consumer Affairs.

6.7. Written Notice from the Collection Agency

By law, the notice from the collection agency (hereafter called "notice") must state the amount of the debt, the name of the creditor, and a statement that you have thirty days to dispute the validity of the debt or the debt will be assumed to be valid.

If you wish to dispute the debt, you must do so in writing within thirty days. The collection agency must then obtain verification of the debt or judgment. The agent must send this verification to you along with the name and address of the original creditor. Until this information is mailed to you, the collection agency cannot attempt to collect.

The notice cannot appear to be a document issued by a court or governmental entity. It cannot appear to be from a law firm or an attorney, unless it really is. They can't simply fake that it is more important than it truly is.

6.8. Threats, Harassment, or Abuse

A collection agency cannot:

1. Threaten violence.
2. Threaten to accuse or accuse someone falsely of fraud or another crime.
3. Tell or threaten to tell a third party that a debt is undisputed if you have disputed the debt in writing.
4. Threaten arrest or the filing of criminal charges for nonpayment where no crime has been committed.
   Special Note: Number 4 does not prevent the filing of hot-check charges if you wrote a check where you didn't have the funds in your account to cover it.
5. Publish a list of debtors who have refused to pay.
6. Advertise the sale of a debt in an attempt to force payment.
7. Threaten to take property without a proper court proceeding UNLESS such property is COLLATERAL.
8. Use profane or obscene language.
9. Phone without disclosing the collection agency's name with willful intent to harass or annoy.
10. Cause the phone to ring repeatedly or make repeated phone calls with intent to harass.
11. Communicate by postcard.
12. Cause you to pay for collect telephone calls without having disclosed the debt collector's name.

6.9. When Calls Can Be Made

By federal law, calls must be made only between the hours of 8 a.m. and 9 p.m. in your time zone.

6.10. Calling You at Work

You can be called at work. If you want to stop this, the next time they call, have your supervisor tell the collection agency that you cannot receive such calls at work. The collection agency must stop or violate the law.

6.11. Getting the Collection Agency to Leave You Alone

If you notify the collection agency in writing that you refuse to pay the debt and that you want the collection agency to end all further contact with you, then all contact must stop. Send this notice certified mail, return receipt requested, so that you can prove it was received. Keep a copy of the letter.

Once you do this, the agency can contact you only to tell you that they will stop all contact or to tell you that a lawsuit will be filed. This is a federal law.

6.12. Penalties for Breaking the Law

If the collection agency breaks a Texas law, there are two possible penalties.

1. Criminal: A conviction of a misdemeanor with a fine of $100–$500. This is very seldom used, but does exist.
2. Civil: A private civil lawsuit can be filed by you and your private attorney.
3. Best Course: Before you try to see the district attorney to file criminal charges or hire an attorney, contact the TEXAS ATTORNEY GENERAL'S OFFICE FOR CONSUMER AFFAIRS. Their services are free. They can file a suit on behalf of the entire state if enough complaints are received.

If a federal law has been broken, you can also file a civil suit through your own attorney. You can recover your actual damages, punitive damages up to $1,000, and attorney's fees. If you are part of a class action suit, the penalties are greater.

Even if you think only a federal law has been violated, file a complaint with the Texas Attorney General's Office. They can help.

True Story

Xavier Anyone, Steven and Trey's cousin, has gotten himself into debt. He had a good job and was able to get several credit cards with high credit limits. Human nature being what it is, he charged to the max. Then Xavier lost his job. He has a new job that doesn't pay very well, and he was out of work for several months. He fell behind in his payments. Now he has a collection agency after him, trying to collect the money. Xavier has no way to pay anything but small installments. He goes to see the attorney for students.

Xavier tells the attorney his sad story. The attorney tells Xavier the information you have just read in this chapter.

Xavier says, "Well, what about the collection agency calling me at home and keeping me on the phone for one hour? It made me late for work. Can I stop that?"

"Why did you let the person keep you on the phone?" asks the lawyer.

"Well, I didn't want to be rude. I had a hard time interrupting. He kept asking me questions and wouldn't believe my answers."

"X, once you have explained your situation to the person, say, 'There is no point in talking any further.' Say goodbye. Then hang up. I know your mother taught you to be polite on the phone, but use some common sense. That man is trained to keep bugging you until you pay. It's silly to let him keep you talking. Interrupt. Say goodbye and HANG UP. There is such a thing as being too polite."

6.13. After a Collection Agency

If unable to collect the money from you, the next step is suing you in a court of law. Generally, this will be in a court in your hometown, unless there is a previous agreement to the contrary, such as a credit cardholder's agreement. You will be served papers by a sheriff's deputy, private process server, or by certified mail.

You have the right to represent yourself, but you may be better off with an attorney to represent you. You will have to hire the attorney yourself. In some cases, if you have a local legal aid office, they may be able to help you.

If it is a debt you owe, you are going to lose with or without an attorney. An attorney can help you if the debt is in dispute. If it is not, an attorney can help you minimize the amount of attorney's fees the creditor can get. Of course, you may not save much in the long run, if you have to pay your own attorney.

6.14. Collecting a Court Judgment

You cannot go to jail for failure to pay a civil court judgment. Under Texas law, a debtor has certain protections. These exceptions do not apply to an order to pay child support or being held in contempt. Both of which may lead to time in jail.

If you own or are buying your home, it CANNOT be taken away to pay a judgment, unless the judgment is for taxes, the mortgage on the home, or for a home-improvement loan on the home. This is the homestead law.

Texas law also allows you to have $30,000 worth of personal property ($60,000 if you are married) that cannot be taken away from you to pay a debt. Personal property is anything but land.

Texas has an additional law that protects your car, furniture, family pictures, children's toys, household pets, and tools of your trade from being seized. These items are added together to reach the $30,000 exemption. These items are NOT protected from seizure if they were used as collateral on a loan.

Wages cannot be garnished. The Texas Supreme Court has held that once you deposit your wages in a checking account, they are no longer "wages" and CAN be taken. The court seems to indicate that you will be left enough money to pay bills but that any excess can be garnished to pay a judgment debt.

Savings accounts, certificates of deposit, and stocks and bonds are NOT protected and can be taken.

6.15. Must the Creditor Attempt to Collect the Judgment?

No. Some creditors put the judgment against your credit, file a lien against any land you own (hoping you own something), and wait. The creditor hopes to receive payment when you are trying to straighten out your credit.

6.16. Interest on a Judgment

The law currently allows a minimum of 10 percent per year on a judgment. This is usually less than the prejudgment interest you were charged on an overdue credit card account.

6.17. Secured Creditor and Repossession

If you borrow money to buy a car, a piece of furniture, a stereo, or a similar item, you almost always sign an agreement to pay the money with the item purchased listed as collateral. This is called a "security agreement." The collateral is the "security" that the loan will be repaid. All security agreements have a paragraph in which you agree that the named item (car, stereo, and so forth) can be taken from you if you fail to pay. This is called "repossession." Texas allows the creditor to take the named item without a court order. You have the right to refuse to let the creditor in the house to repossess your stereo, though.

If you do so, the creditor must get a court order to allow entry to seize the stereo. You can be made to pay the creditor's cost of obtaining that court order if so stated in the terms of your loan agreement.

You must be given a reasonable period of time to pay the entire amount of the note (not just catch up on payments due). If you do not pay to redeem the item, it will be sold. The sale proceeds must be applied to the amount you owe and costs of the sale.

Special Note 1: Sale proceeds of used merchandise almost never cover the entire amount due. You will still owe the remaining balance.

Special Note 2: BEWARE of making late payments. Just because the creditor allowed a late payment last time DOES NOT mean he or she will allow it this time. Under most agreements, the creditor reserves the right to repossess ANYTIME you are late or delinquent, EVEN though he or she didn't do it the first time.

Consumer Concerns and Other Issues

6.18. Three-Day Right to Cancel a Written Contract

You have the right to cancel certain contracts even though you signed them.

Home-solicitation contracts for $25 or more can be canceled. Notify the other party in the manner noted on the contract that you wish to cancel. You have three business days after signing. Always do so in writing and send it certified mail, return receipt requested, so that you can prove it was received. Keep a copy of your letter. Be sure it will be postmarked by midnight of the third business day.

Home-solicitation contracts clearly include door-to-door sales. Whether such contracts include telephone or internet sales is not clear. It is safest to assume they do not, so don't rely on the three-day right to cancel for phone or internet sales. Also, the three-day right to cancel does not include a door-to-door salesman who gives you a coupon that you must go into his business place to use. The sale is then taking place in a store, not your home.

Health-spa and gym contracts also must have the three-day right-to-cancel clause, even though they are not a "home solicitation."

6.19. Health-Spa and Gym Contracts

State law regulates health-spa contracts by requiring certain clauses in the contract and forbidding certain practices.

The contract must contain the following clauses or paragraphs set forth in bold print.

1. Three-day right to cancel: As noted in § 6.18 above, the contract must contain this right with instructions on how to do it. Be sure to send the notice certified mail, return receipt requested, and be sure to send it on time.

2. Health-spa or gym closing: If the health-spa or gym CLOSES, it must send you a statement telling you where to send notice of your cancellation. This cancellation right doesn't exist if the spa or gym provides you with another similar facility that will accept your membership with no transfer fee and that is within ten miles of the old spa or gym.

3. Your poor health, injury, or death: In case of disability or death, the contract can be canceled. The spa/gym may require proof of disability or death. A prorated refund will be made if the fees have already been paid in full.

If the contract does not contain these three clauses in bold print, you can cancel the contract. The spa or gym may be subject to other penalties as well.

6.20. Refunds on Merchandise

There is no law that requires a business to give you a refund if you decide you don't want the item, whether it is five minutes after you buy it or two weeks later. No refund need be made.

Many large businesses will refund your money if you decide you don't like the color, but many will not. It is very common for smaller businesses to offer an exchange or credit in the store rather than a refund. They don't even have to do that. *There is no requirement that a sign be posted stating this policy or that the receipt have the policy printed on it.*

If a new item is defective, you MUST be offered a refund. If it is a used item, there is no requirement to refund. You buy a used item as is.

Electronics stores, ski equipment stores, and the like seldom give refunds. Before you make the purchase, be sure you really want and can afford the item.

True Story

Steven has some really amazing stereo equipment in his car, but he'd like to upgrade it. A local stereo store advertises the very speakers he wants at a special sale price. It will take all of his spare cash, but they will be worth it.

Steven goes to the store, talks to the salesman, and examines the advertised speakers. Steven gets into a technical discussion with the salesman. He tells the salesman what results he expects, using the new speakers. The salesman says that Steven will be disappointed with them because they won't do what Steven wants. What Steven really needs is a different set of speakers that costs more and is not on sale (naturally).

Steven is very disappointed. He really wanted to upgrade his equipment. He'd already told all of his friends how it was going to sound. Now he'll have to confess he was wrong about what was advertised.

The salesman offers Steven a really good deal on the more expensive speakers. Steven hesitates. It still costs more than the advertised price, but it is a good deal and his stereo will sound great. In short, he talks himself into it.

As he is carrying the boxes to his car, he has second thoughts. What will he eat for the next month? He's spent all of his food money plus his spare cash on these speakers. Common sense reasserts itself, and Steven realizes that he has made a mistake. He turns around and returns to the store with the unopened boxes in his arms. It has been almost one minute since he paid.

Steven asks for his money back, explaining his problem. To his horror, the cashier points to the sign on the cash register. "No refunds." It also says that on his receipt. They will exchange the merchandise for something else, but he can't have his money back.

Unfortunately, Steven will have to get his nourishment from great-sounding music for the next month. The store does not have to give a refund, since the merchandise was not defective.

6.21. Layaways

Many stores offer this service. Be sure you understand the terms of this agreement. Know how often you must make a payment and how long the layaway lasts.

If you miss a payment, the item can be returned to the shelf and sold to someone else for the full price. You are not entitled to a refund of any sort.

Pick up layaways promptly once the final payment is made. Stores are not in the free-storage business.

6.22. Late Billings

If a bill comes late, do you still have to pay? YES! If your cell phone company bills you for the first time one year after you made the long-distance calls, YOU STILL OWE THE MONEY. If the first bill is more than four years late, then you can claim that the bill is passed the statute of limitations. Remember, that only means they can't win if they take you to court. The company can still shut your service down, and it can still go against your credit.

6.23. Credit Card Responsibility

It is very unwise to lend your credit or debit card to anyone, even your best friend. If you give your friend permission to use the credit card to buy gas, and he or she uses it for other things as well, you may be responsible for those additional purchases if your friend does not pay you.

If your credit or debit card is lost or stolen, you are responsible for only $50 of the purchases made by the thief. You must notify the credit card company of the loss or theft as soon as possible. Some credit/debit card companies may even waive this $50 fee.

It is wise to be very careful about using your credit or debit card for telephone or internet purchases. While many such companies are reputable, some are not. Sometimes products are not as represented. Sometimes the amount billed to your credit card is more than the amount you authorized. If you call the seller, it is unlikely you will experience such problems.

Credit card machines have come a long way. Always check to make sure your receipt only has the last few numbers of your credit/debit card printed on it. If your copy or the merchant copy has your full credit card number on it, anyone can see it. If someone sees it, he or she can steal it and use it for online purchases. Your credit/debit card number is like your social security number. Keep it to yourself, and DON'T SHARE IT. If you have the ability to get the chip in your credit/debit card, do so. This is just one more step in the security of your card.

If you do have a problem with a merchant on a card purchase, first attempt to correct the problem with the merchant. If you are not satisfied, you may contact your credit/debit card company, or bank, for assistance if:

1. The purchase is for more than $50.
2. The purchase is made in your home state or within one hundred miles of your mailing address.

Even if you don't meet those conditions, try your credit/debit card company. They may be willing to help.

Remember, you must notify the credit card company about billing errors, in writing, within sixty days of receiving the bill.

It is a FELONY to use a credit card without the owner's permission.

6.24. Power of Attorney

This is a piece of paper signed in front of a notary public in which you give someone the power to act for you. A notary public is someone qualified to verify that people who sign forms or documents are who they say they are. A notary public can be anyone eighteen years old or older.

A general power of attorney means that the person you have named as your "power of attorney" can sign your name and in general do anything on your behalf. This person could sell your car, pay your bills from your account, and so forth. Obviously, you only name someone you trust.

A *special* power of attorney is a document that empowers your "power of attorney" to do only a specific act, like sell your car.

Forms for this can be obtained from any large office supply company that has legal forms or you may download from the internet. Make sure you get one for the State of Texas.

A power of attorney can be for a specific stated period of time or for an indefinite time—that is, until you revoke it.

Powers of attorney do not need to be registered anywhere to be valid, but you can register a power of attorney with the county clerk. If you do register it, then you must revoke it in writing and register the revocation. If you don't register it, you can revoke it by tearing it up.

The person (the power of attorney) who is going to use the power of attorney on your behalf must have the original, notarized document. A copy will not do.

6.25. Certified Mail Return Receipt Requested

Use this type of mail to prove that the mailed item is received. Address your envelope in the ordinary manner, but do not put a stamp on it. Go to any post office window and ask for this service. It costs less than five dollars. You will be asked to fill out a postcard with your name and address on it. This postcard will be returned to you with the receiver's signature. It proves the letter was received.

If you get a notice at home telling you to come to the post office to pick up a certified letter, DO SO. If you fail to, by law you are presumed to have received it. You are responsible for its contents. IT NEVER HARMS YOU TO PICK UP THE LETTER. It may harm you greatly if you don't pick it up.

Chapter 7

LIVING ON YOUR OWN

Hopefully, it won't be long until you are out of your parents' home and living on your own. But realize, living on your own presents an entirely new set of rights, responsibilities, and problems. Since you will most likely rent the first place you live, this chapter will set forth the rights, responsibilities, and problems of renting an apartment or house. Although I'll frequently refer to an "apartment," because that is the most common first rental residence, the same rules apply to a duplex or house. If you are moving into a dorm, it will have rules of its own that will not be covered here. Trust me, the rules of your dorm room will be drilled into you by your resident assistant (RA).

Leases

7.1. The Oral Lease

The oral or verbal lease is an agreement that is not written down. Most are simple agreements about the amount of rent and deposit.

Oral agreements can have other clauses, such as how long you will live in the apartment, no pets, maintenance of yard, and so forth.

Oral leases have at least two major problems:

1. If no agreement is made on the length of time you will live in the apartment, the landlord only has to give you a thirty-day notice to change anything. He or she can give you a thirty-day notice and raise the rent, tell you to move for no reason, tell you to get rid of a roommate or a pet. You have one advantage in this type of agreement: to move out, you must only give a thirty-day notice.
2. People can easily misunderstand the terms of the original agreement or fail to remember exactly what was said. This can create major problems and may end up costing you money.

Example: You say you never agreed to live in the apartment for a specific period of time. After four months, you give a thirty-day notice that you will be moving out at the end of the fifth month. The landlord says you agreed to live in the apartment for six months and cannot move until the sixth month is up. With nothing in writing, it's a swearing match. If the landlord takes you to court for the rent for the sixth month, who will the judge or jury believe?

The bottom line is that the problems with oral leases outweigh any advantages. If the choice is up to you, it is better to insist on a written lease. If the landlord doesn't have a lease form, you can download one from the internet, purchase one for a small sum from an office supply business that sells legal forms, or you could draw up your agreement yourself on ordinary paper in plain English. As long as it clearly states the agreement in ink and *is dated and signed by you and the landlord*, it will be considered to be a binding document.

7.2. When Is It Okay to Have an Oral Lease?

When your written lease has expired and the landlord does not ask you to sign a new lease, it is probably okay not to insist on a written lease. You know the landlord; the landlord knows you. It is not likely under these conditions that the landlord will raise your rent each month or give you notice to move for no reason. However, he or she could if they wanted to.

Special Note: Sometimes certain terms of the lease carry forward, even though the lease has ended.

7.3. Month-to-Month Lease

The term "month-to-month" means that you have not agreed to live in the apartment for any specific length of time. You pay rent monthly; you can give a thirty-day notice to move or be given a thirty-day notice to move, at any time. Usually, month-to-month tenancies are oral, but they can be written.

7.4. The Law and Oral Leases

If the oral agreement is month to month and doesn't cover certain things, the law steps in. For instance, the law says you must give one rent period notice if you wish to move, unless you have agreed otherwise. This means, if you pay rent by the month, you must give one month's notice (thirty days). If there is no agreement to the contrary, you can give this notice on any day of the month. If you give notice on May 11, then you can move out June 11. You pay only eleven days of rent in June. This is called "prorated rent" and is calculated by dividing one month's rent by thirty to find the daily rate. Take the daily rate and multiply it by the number of days to give you the correct prorated amount.

Example of prorated rent: Let's say your rent is $500 per month, and you are going to stay in the apartment for eleven days. Five hundred dollars (rent) / divided by thirty (days in the month) equals $16.66. This amount ($16.66) is what you pay per day for that apartment. Multiply it by eleven (the days you are staying). Eleven times $16.66 equals $183.26. This amount is how much you pay for rent for those eleven days.

With an oral lease, notices of move-out and needed repairs DO NOT have to be in writing, unless you have previously agreed that they will be. It is still a good idea to give these notices in writing, so there can be no confusion on when and whether they were given. If you give any notice to your landlord, always keep a copy. Date your notice.

Certain other laws also apply, including laws concerning repair, eviction, deadbolt locks, deposit refund, ownership disclosure, and others. These will be discussed at length below, after the WRITTEN LEASE section, because the laws apply to both oral and written leases.

7.5. Written Lease

This document can be as simple as a handwritten paper setting forth the amount of rent for a fixed period of time, or as complicated as a lawyer-drawn, multipage document in small print.

To be legal, the lease MUST be dated and signed by both the landlord and the tenant.

You are entitled to a copy of the lease. The typical lease includes names of all parties, the length of time that you will live in the apartment, how much rent is owed and on what day, whether pets are allowed, how to notify the landlord for repairs, the deposit amount, and how much notice is required before moving out.

The main rules to remember are:

1. READ THE LEASE BEFORE SIGNING IT. (I know it's long, boring, and the landlord is standing at your elbow, but READ it anyway. Remember Rules to Live By number 7? Never sign anything if you don't understand what you are signing.) This will save you from nasty surprises later on.
2. Be sure all blanks are filled in properly.
3. A printed lease CAN BE ALTERED or changed, if all parties agree to it and initial and date the changes.
4. A printed lease can be added to, in writing, above the signatures, if initialed. A separate piece of paper for additions can be used if everyone signs and dates it.

Special Note: Almost all written leases have a clause that says NO ORAL AGREEMENTS are valid. This means that oral promise of new carpet CANNOT be enforced unless you put it IN WRITING.

Below is a step-by-step guide to finding, renting, living in, and moving out of an apartment.

Looking for an Apartment

*7.6. Finding an Apartment

You already know how to do an online search, how to check the classified sections of your newspaper and the phone book's yellow pages under "apartments." You may not be aware of several other "helps."

1. Free apartment finders: Many cities have businesses whose function is helping you find the right apartment. They are usually listed in the phone book under "apartments." They can save you lots of telephoning and are free. If you rent an apartment through such an agency, your landlord pays them.

2. Apartment associations: Many larger cities have an association that prints a guide to members' apartments. This guide is free. You may find a brochure in the foyer of the grocery or convenience store.

3. Tenant associations: Some major cities have tenant associations who may print a guide.

4. University or college guide: If you are a student at a university or college, check with your student government to see if they provide a guide.

5. Chamber of Commerce: Just about every city, large or small, has a chamber of commerce. Most likely, they will have apartment listings too.

An asterisk (*) before the section number and title means that the section applies to oral as well as written leases.

*7.7. Discrimination

It is illegal to refuse to rent to a person based on race, religion, country of national origin, or family status. If you believe you have been discriminated against in renting or in being evicted, contact the property owner first. If that does not resolve the situation, you can contact your local civil rights council, the Texas Workforce Commission (address and phone numbers listed in section § 6.2), or HUD—Fair Housing and Equal Opportunity (FHED).

You may contact HUD—Fair Housing and Equal Opportunity (FHED) home office by calling (1-888) 560-8913 or make a complaint online at: https://portal.hud.gov/hudportal/HUD.

If you would like to make a complaint in person, you must do that in one of only three offices in Texas. They are:

Fort Worth
801 Cherry Street, Unit 45
Suite 2500
Ft. Worth, Texas 76102
(817) 978-5600

Houston
1301 Fannin, Suite 2200
Houston, Texas 77002
(713) 718-3199
San Antonio

Hipolito F. Garcia Federal Building
615 East Houston Street, Suite 347
San Antonio, Texas 78205-2001
(210) 475-6806

*7.8. Viewing Your Apartment

Ask to see the apartment that you may actually be living in. The law requires that a vacating tenant (the tenant moving out) allow his or her apartment to be shown. If the apartment is still occupied, it may be hard to imagine what you will be getting. Notice the floors, walls, countertops, appliances, and any furniture that will be yours. In most cases, WHAT YOU SEE IS WHAT YOU GET. If the landlord promises paint, new carpet, or curtains, GET IT IN WRITING so that you can enforce it. If the landlord WON'T put it in writing, the odds are that he or she is not certain that you will get new carpet. If the new carpet is important to you, DO NOT TAKE THE APARTMENT.

In older houses or apartments, notice evidence of prior problems, especially with plumbing. Evidence of water leaks under the sink or on the ceiling should cause you to closely question the landlord. Have repairs been made? Ask the current tenant. I will say it again, WHAT YOU SEE IS WHAT YOU GET, especially in an older building.

*7.9. Beware of Model Apartments

Some apartments have a "model" apartment for you to view. No one has ever lived in this apartment, so it will be in perfect condition. Ask to see your actual apartment. If the landlord will not show it to you, you have to make a difficult choice. If the apartment complex is an older one, BEWARE. Your actual apartment may have many battle scars. If the complex is new, there is a better chance that your apartment will not disappoint you. The decision is yours.

7.10. Applications to Rent

Once you have seen the apartment and want to rent it, some landlords will require you to fill out an application to rent. This is the landlord's opportunity to check you out. The application will ask for financial information and references from previous landlords. Under most rental applications, once you sign the application, YOU HAVE AGREED TO RENT the apartment. The landlord is not bound to offer you the apartment, but you are required to accept it if he or she does offer it to you. DON'T FILL OUT AND SIGN THE APPLICATION unless you intend to rent the apartment.

*7.11. Deposit

Most landlords will require that you pay a deposit at the time you fill out the application. If there is no application, you will pay the deposit at the time you say you want to rent the apartment. This is called a "security deposit." When it is paid in advance, it is really a "holding" deposit. If there is no application, the deposit serves also as evidence of your agreement to rent the apartment. In return, the landlord agrees to hold the apartment for you and not rent it to someone else.

If you move in, this "holding" deposit becomes a "security" deposit to guarantee that you will abide by the rules in the lease and won't damage any property. More about that function later.

ALWAYS GET A RECIEPT!

If you DON'T move in, YOU MAY LOSE ALL OR PART OF YOUR DEPOSIT. If the landlord finds a replacement tenant who moves in on or before the date your lease was to begin, the landlord must refund your deposit, but he or she can keep a cancellation fee if stated in the lease, or may withhold the actual expenses incurred in finding the new tenant.

If you find a replacement tenant acceptable to the landlord, you will get a refund of your full deposit. If no acceptable tenant is found, you will lose your ENTIRE DEPOSIT.

DON'T PAY A DEPOSIT UNLESS YOU ARE SURE THAT YOU WANT THE APARTMENT.

*7.12. Utilities

When pricing apartments to fit your budget, don't forget utilities. Some apartments are "all bills paid"; most are not. Ask the landlord what the average utility bill will be and add a $50 cushion. Most landlords tend to underestimate utility costs. If you want a really accurate amount, ask the tenant who is moving out. You should also check with utility companies to find out if you are required to post a deposit to begin service. If you have never had utilities in your name before, you will most likely have to pay a deposit.

7.13. All Residents Should Sign the Lease

This is for your protection as much as the landlord's. Most leases have a "joint and several liabilities" clause. This is a legal phrase that means that each person who signs the lease is responsible to the landlord for the full amount of the rent, not just his or her one-half or one-third. It is better for the tenants to have all tenants legally bound to pay rent, not just one or two. If only one name is on the lease, that is the person the landlord will sue if the lease is broken. You don't want to be sued alone. Also, if a dispute arises between tenants, the one on the lease may be able to lock out any tenants who are not on the lease.

7.14. Length of the Lease

Don't sign a lease that goes until May 2019 if you plan to move out in December 2018. There can be serious consequences to breaking a lease by moving out early. They will be discussed in §§ 7.42–7.49. Shop around until you find the right length of time at the right kind of apartment. Be sure the correct length of time gets filled in on the lease so that there won't be any surprises later. DO NOT buy the landlord's story that he or she will let you out early, even though you must sign a lease for a longer period of time. The landlord may get run over by a truck tomorrow, and nobody else will know anything about your "special" move-out deal. Besides, you now know that most leases have that "no oral agreements" clause.

True Story

Theresa Anyone is thinking of moving out of her apartment. She wants to be sure to get back her deposit. She goes to see the attorney for students at her college for advice. (This attorney's advice is free.)

The attorney says, "How long is your lease?"

Theresa answers by holding her hands up about fourteen inches apart. (She is showing the attorney the length of the paper the lease is written on!)

The attorney closes her eyes and stifles her laughter. "Earth to Theresa. Earth to Theresa," she says. "How long are you supposed to live in the apartment?"

"Oh," Theresa says. "I don't know. The usual time, I guess."

"Theresa, come back with the lease. I can't help you until I see what it says."

"Okay, if I can find it," says Theresa.

The lawyer thinks to herself as Theresa leaves, "Do you suppose she knows to look before crossing the street, or is she really from some other planet?"

*7.15. Pets

Be sure your lease says that pets are permitted if you've been told you can have one. Some leases have a "no pets" clause that must be crossed out and initialed. No landlord has to allow pets, so it's up to the landlord to regulate the size, weight, and type of pet permitted.

The landlord can also charge a pet fee or deposit. Be sure you understand whether the amount you pay is a refundable deposit or a nonrefundable fee or a combination.

If you pay a deposit, have a pet, and then get rid of the pet, don't be surprised if the landlord refuses to refund the deposit until you vacate the apartment. The landlord needs an empty apartment to assess damage and to see if it needs defleaing.

Living in an Apartment

*7.16. Move-In Inventory 1

Some apartments provide a form for this. Some don't. If there is no form provided, use a piece of paper. Room by room, write down any existing damage, such as marks or holes in the wall, stains on floors, carpet, or countertops, torn shades or curtains, cracked windows, and chipped appliances. If it comes furnished, check out the furniture. Date and sign the list, then copy it. Give the landlord one copy to attach to your lease, and you keep the other. Use that smartphone and take pictures. As a matter of fact, take lots of pictures. You do not need to provide pictures to the landlord. If you have to go to court later, you will be glad you have them. Make sure the function on your phone is turned on to record time and date of each photo.

A MOVE-IN INVENTORY AND PICTURES KEEP YOU FROM HAVING TO PAY FOR SOMEONE ELSE'S DAMAGE when you move out. They avoid fights over your deposit refund (see § 7.55 Move-In Inventory 2).

*7.17. Pay Your Rent on Time

It saves you trouble and money in the long run. It also makes good points with the landlord that might come in handy later on. If you pay rent after the due date and grace period, if there is a grace period, there is almost always a penalty. Read the lease to see what the late charges will be. Under most leases, failure or refusal to pay late fees can result in the late fees being deducted from your next month's rent. You will then have to pay the remaining amount of rent due or be evicted.

*7.18. Hot Checks

Try to avoid this, but if you write a check to your landlord and it is no good, because you don't have the money in the account, be aware that you will have to pay a hot-check fee of up to $25. IN ADDITION, you will have to pay LATE CHARGES, because a hot check means the rent wasn't paid on time. Late charges run from the date rent was due until you pay it. As noted above, in most leases, if you refuse to pay the hot-check fee or late fee, it can be deducted from next month's rent. You will then have to pay the balance due on the rent or be evicted.

*7.19. Never Refuse to Pay Rent

In Texas, it is illegal to refuse to pay rent under almost all circumstances. Just about the only reason you can refuse to pay rent is if you can't live in the apartment because of fire or tornado damage. YOU CANNOT REFUSE TO PAY RENT because A REPAIR HAS NOT BEEN MADE.

*7.20. Deadbolt Locks

You may require that the landlord install a new lock or change or rekey the old lock. Check your lease to see if this request must be in writing. Normally, the landlord has seven days to honor your request. In some circumstances, a longer time may be okay. The landlord can require your roommates to approve the change. If a burglary, attempted burglary, or crime of personal violence has occurred at the apartment complex, the landlord must honor your request within seventy-two hours. The landlord can CHARGE THE COST TO YOU, unless the door or window has no lock on it at all or if it is a sliding glass door without a pin lock. You can be charged the costs of labor, EVEN IF the work is done by the landlord's maintenance man. If the landlord fails to fulfill your request, you may rekey or replace the lock and deduct the actual cost from the next month's rent. Attach a copy of the receipt to the next month's rent check. You may also seek a court order to make him or her do so and obtain a judgment against the landlord for any actual damages that you have incurred, plus one month's rent, plus $500, plus court costs and attorney's fees, AND you can terminate the lease.

*7.21. Smoke Alarms

State law requires that all rented dwellings have a working smoke alarm. If it is battery operated, the battery must be working when you move in. During the time you live in the apartment, you must replace the battery if it wears out. If the alarm needs repair, the landlord must repair it, if you report it. If the landlord fails to install or repair a smoke alarm, you can get a court order requiring installation or repair, plus any damages you have suffered, plus one month's rent, court costs, attorney's fees, plus one hundred dollars. You can also terminate the lease.

*7.22. Noise

When you live in an apartment or duplex, you are sharing very close living space with your neighbors. You have rights, but so do they. Loud noise at an unreasonable hour is a CRIME, as well as a violation of your lease. Act responsibly and avoid trouble.

If too much noise is being made, the manager or landlord should be contacted, if contacting the noisemakers directly has not worked. If that doesn't solve the problem, the police are the next step.

The law says making too much noise at an unreasonable hour and disturbing your neighbors is disorderly conduct. You are subject to arrest and a fine of up to $500. If it is a party, then the party host is responsible for the noise level of his or her guests. The host is the one who will pay the fine or go to jail and may even be evicted.

*7.23. Damages

Under most leases, written or oral, you are responsible to pay for any damage caused by you or your guests. If you refuse to pay, most written leases allow the landlord to apply rent paid by you to other amounts owed first. The landlord will apply the rent to the damages and then bill you for more rent. You must pay or be evicted.

Remember, the landlord DOES NOT have to allow you to make the repair. The landlord can insist that it be made by a professional or his or her maintenance person.

7.24. Parking

Most leases contain a statement that the landlord regulates all parking. Those regulations can change during the course of your lease if you are given notice. Be sure that you know what the regulations are so that you won't be towed.

*7.25. Owner's Name

By law, the manager must give you the owner's name and address and the management company's name and address if you request it. Read your lease. Some leases require that you make this request in writing. The manager has seven days to provide this information. In the alternative, the manager can choose to keep the information posted in or near the office or provide the information with your lease.

If the manager fails to provide the information after the seven days, you can get a court order requiring the landlord to disclose the information. You can also get a judgment against the landlord for damages, one month's rent, plus one hundred dollars, court costs, and attorney's fees. You can also terminate the lease.

*7.26. Utility Interruptions

Utilities can be interrupted in two ways, and the solution to the problem is different in each case.

1. When you pay utilities: The landlord CANNOT interrupt the utilities except for repairs, construction, or an emergency. If the landlord violates this, you may terminate the lease and recover from the landlord actual damages, one month's rent or $500, whichever is greater, and reasonable attorney's fees and court costs, less any delinquent rents.
2. When the landlord pays utilities: If you get a notice from the utility company that the utility will be cut off for nonpayment by the landlord, you can:
   a) Pay the utility company and deduct from your rent the amount paid. Be sure to provide a receipt for this to the landlord.
   b) Terminate the lease with written notice within thirty days of when you get notice from the utility of a future cutoff or actual cutoff; you may deduct your security deposit from the rent and recover a pro-rata refund or any advance rent.
   c) Sue in court for actual damages including moving costs, reconnection fees, storage fees, and lost wages, along with court costs and attorney's fees.

*7.27. Property or Renter's Insurance

GET SOME! As a general rule, the landlord is NOT responsible if you are burglarized, have a fire, have water pipes burst, or have a severe roof leak. The landlord is responsible if the problem occurs because of the landlord's negligence. The landlord is negligent if the fire starts in his or her boiler room where newspapers were stored, but not if your next-door neighbor has a grease fire. The landlord is negligent if you have reported the lack of locks on your windows and that's how the burglar got in. If the burglar kicked in the locked front door, the landlord is not negligent. The first time the pipes burst or the roof leaks, the landlord is not negligent. If it is the second or third time for the leaks, and faulty repairs have been made in between leaks, then the landlord may be negligent.

The bottom line is that most losses are your problem, not the landlord's. Renter's or property insurance covers the cost to replace your property and is cheaper than you think. It can also be a real lifesaver. Most insurance companies sell "Renter's Insurance." This insurance is usually sold in $1,000 increments, which is $1,000, $2,000, $3,000, and so forth, worth of coverage. If you have $5,000 worth of property in your apartment, get $5,000 worth of renter's insurance. You may have to talk to several companies before you find one that is willing to sell you a policy for the amount of coverage you want. Remember, insurance pays VALUE OF THE ITEM DESTROYED, NOT REPLACEMENT COST. If you want replacement cost, it is usually available for an extra fee.

Special Note: DO NOT ASSUME that your PARENTS' homeowner's policy automatically covers you if you live away from home. Check it out. Many homeowner policies cover you if you're a student living in a dorm but not if you live off campus in a house or apartment.

*7.28. Furnishing Your Apartment

Milk crates, cinder blocks, and wooden boards are a great way to create bookcases or other storage. However, don't be tempted to take lumber, bricks, or cinder blocks from construction sites without permission. This is THEFT. The seriousness of the theft depends on how much you steal. An amount under one hundred dollars is a Class C misdemeanor, punishable by a $500 fine. From $101 to less than $750 is a Class B misdemeanor, punishable by a fine of up to $2,000 and/or up to six months in jail.

You would be surprised how few cinder blocks and two-by-fours it takes to equal one hundred dollars. You will be arrested if caught. When I say "if caught," that does not mean go after dark like a ninja. It means don't steal them.

*7.29. Landlord's Right to Enter

He or she can enter at all reasonable times for any legitimate purpose. He or she is NOT required to give you advance notice that he or she will enter, UNLESS it is so stated in your lease. You can NEVER change the locks and refuse to give the landlord a key. You are only the renter. The landlord is either the owner or represents the owner and must be allowed entry. You CANNOT insist that the landlord enter only when you are there.

Repairs

It is illegal to refuse to pay rent because the landlord has not made repairs. In most cases, it is also illegal to make repairs on your own and deduct the charges from your rent. Below are some steps that are legal.

*7.30. Giving Notice on Needed Repairs

Always give notice of needed repairs in writing, note the date, and keep a copy. This prevents later arguments over whether notice was given and when it was given. This first notice determines all further steps that you can take to get repairs made. Besides, most leases require that the notice be in writing. Remember, pictures always help if a court date is in your future.

Most landlords will repair if all they receive is oral notice, in spite of what the lease says. The one time you rely on the oral notice and give no written notice is bound to be the time the repair does not get made. If your lease requires written notice, the landlord has a legal excuse for not having made the repair. So, bottom line: GIVE WRITTEN DATED NOTICE.

Special Note: Call in emergencies, but follow with a written notice.

True Story

Theresa has decided to stay in her apartment, if she can get the heater "fixed." She notifies the manager in writing that the heater does not adequately heat the back bedroom. The maintenance man comes but can find nothing wrong with the heater. Theresa and the manager go round and round, arguing about the heater. The manager says the heater is working properly. Theresa says that she is still cold.

Finally, Theresa goes to see the attorney for students again. This time she remembers to bring her lease. (Of course, this time it isn't needed.) She explains the problem.

"Let me get this straight," says the attorney. "The heater is working, but your bedroom is too cold."

"Right," says Theresa. "You see, the heater and air conditioner are combined in a single unit, mounted in the living room window."

"You mean, the hot air just blows out of that unit. There are no heating ducts to the bedroom?" asks the lawyer.

"Right," says Theresa.

"So, you want the landlord to add heating ducts for the bedroom?"

"Right! It's too cold," says Theresa.

"Theresa, that is not a repair. That is asking for an alteration to the apartment. Even if the bedroom is too cold for you, the landlord has no duty to change the heating system. You rented the apartment with that type of heater, so you are stuck with it," says the lawyer. "The landlord is not required to alter it. There has been no breach of the lease."

*7.31. How Much Time Does the Landlord Have to Make a Repair?

He or she has "reasonable" time. What is "reasonable?" It depends on the problem. If the dishwasher won't work, three or four weeks is reasonable. If you have no water, no hot water, or no working toilet, one or two days is reasonable. It really depends on the seriousness of the problem and the availability of parts and labor. If the heater is broken, but it is May, the landlord has more time to fix it than he or she would have in January. If you think reasonable time has lapsed, call the landlord to find out what the holdup is.

*7.32. If Reasonable Time Has Lapsed and the Repair Has Not Been Made

1. Go over the head of the local manager to his or her supervisor, the management company, or the apartment owner. Remember, you have a RIGHT to the owner's and management company's names and addresses.
2. Complain to the local apartment association if your landlord is a member.
3. Complain to the local tenant's association if there is one.
4. If you are a student at a college or university that provides a legal counselor for students, enlist that person's help.
5. Complain in writing to the local Better Business Bureau and to the nearest Texas Attorney General's Office for Consumer Affairs (see § 8.62 and § 8.63 for details).
6. If the above remedies fail, there is a law that sets forth a procedure to follow. You send a SECOND notice of repair, giving the landlord seven days to make the repair. If he or she fails to do so, you can cancel the lease and move out, getting back your deposit and prorated rent, IF the needed repair is MATERIAL TO YOUR HEALTH OR SAFETY. What does "material to your health or safety" mean? In this case, "material" means IMPORTANT, so the phrase means "important to your health or safety." This could include broken door locks, broken toilets, no heat in the winter, no air conditioning in the summer, and so forth. This

means you can't cancel the lease because the dishwasher is broken or the faucet is dripping and repairs haven't been made.

7. If you don't want to move out, the law allows you to sue the landlord for a court to order the landlord to:
   a) Make the repair.
   b) Reduce your rent until the repair is made.
   c) Pay your actual damages, court costs, and attorney's fees.
   d) Pay you a penalty of one month's rent plus $500.

   Special Note: Suing your landlord is a last resort. You may win your case, but you may make the landlord very angry. Future relations may be unpleasant. Be sure that you are willing to live with this unpleasantness before you sue.

8. When you can make the repair and deduct it from your rent:
   a) If the landlord so agrees.
   b) If the landlord has failed to remedy the backup of raw sewage inside the apartment or the flooding from broken pipes or natural drainage, and you've given notice of your intent to repair.
   c) If the landlord has agreed to furnish water but you have none, and three days have lapsed since notice that you would make the repair.
   d) If the landlord has agreed to furnish heating or cooling and it is not working properly, and the landlord has been notified in writing by the appropriate local authority (housing, building, or health) that the lack of heat or cooling materially affects your health or safety, and three days have lapsed since giving notice of your intent to repair.
   e) If an appropriate official has notified the landlord that the condition materially affects the health or safety of an ordinary tenant, and seven days have passed since you gave the landlord notice of your intent to repair.

Such repairs must be made by a professional, not by you or your relatives (unless the landlord agrees). You cannot have repairs made that cost more than the amount of rent you owe. You must provide receipts to the landlord. To invoke any of these remedies, you must owe no back rent.

*7.33. Legal Delay of Repair

The landlord can give a sworn statement (affidavit) to the tenant to legally delay his or her duty to repair:

1. For fifteen days if the delay is caused by obtaining necessary parts for which the landlord is not at fault.
2. For thirty days if the delay is caused by a general shortage of labor or materials following a natural disaster, such as tornado or hurricane.

*7.34. Landlord Can Sue You

If you refuse to pay rent because repairs have not been made or you deduct the cost of repairs improperly from your rent, the landlord can sue you for actual damages and one month's rent plus $500.

Roommates

The landlord-tenant laws say nothing about roommates. Leases usually do. As stated earlier, all people who sign the lease are responsible to see that all of the rent gets paid to the landlord, not just that person's one-half or one-third. The agreement to share rent, space, and other bills is between the roommates only. It does not involve the landlord. The landlord usually retains the right to insist on a single check for rent payment, and he or she may issue only one deposit refund check after you move out. Notice of intent to move out is usually treated as notice from all roommates, even if it is only signed by one. The landlord can treat you as one family.

Other problems that may arise between roommates are as follows.

* 7.35 Nonpayment of Bills

All too often, one deadbeat roommate takes advantage of responsible roommates by not paying his or her share of the bills. If it is rent, the unpaid balance must be paid, or all roommates may be evicted. If it is the electric bill, the bill must be paid to continue service. The utility company expects payment from the person whose name is on the bill.

To avoid or minimize these problems, try the following. Don't get all of the bills in one roommate's name. You get the electric bill in your name, and let your roommate get the water in his or her name. Then you have a hold on each other. If a deposit must be posted to get utility service, all roommates should contribute equally. If a guarantor is going to guarantee payment of the water bill, instead of posting a deposit, get the water in your name, BUT get your roommate's parents to guarantee the bill. That way both families are involved.

If you do get stuck with your roommate's part of the bill, you can sue your roommate in small claims court. Unfortunately, that is not a very good solution (see § 8.11 on small claims court for further information).

*7.36. Lending Money

DON'T. REALLY, I MEAN DON'T . . . EVER. Avoid this problem by refusing to lend money, especially if it is a large amount. Deadbeat roommates will never pay you back. Since it is difficult to tell the deadbeats from the good guys, play it safe. Don't lend money or at least don't lend an amount that you can't afford to lose.

*7.37. Sharing Space

If you've never lived with this person before, it's a good idea to lay down some ground rules. Be smart and put them in writing. Areas to cover in your agreement are:

1. Paying bills.
2. Who uses what bedrooms, bathrooms, and shelves in the refrigerator.
3. Whether you're willing to share food, stereo, TV, PlayStation, or clothes.

4. Whether a boyfriend or girlfriend can sleep over or not, and if so, for how many days a week.

You can probably think of other areas, too. An agreement from the beginning can save arguments later.

*7.38. Moving Out Early

If your roommate disappears and the rent is due, you will have to pay the entire amount or move. The landlord might be willing to give you some extra time to pay the rent or find a new roommate if you've been a good tenant.

If you have to move, you will lose your deposit. The landlord can sue either of you or both of you.

If you stay and pay the extra rent, you can sue your ex-roommate for it, but collecting the money may be difficult (see § 8.11 on small claims court).

*7.39. Buying Things Together

I mean sofas, appliances, TVs, and so forth. It is probably better not to, but if you do, write an agreement at the beginning. The agreement should say how you are going to pay for the item and how you are going to divide the item when you move out. A written agreement can save headaches later.

*7.40. Getting Rid of a Deadbeat Roommate

Legally, you cannot evict a roommate whose name is on the lease, deny him or her entry to the apartment, or hold property of that roommate hostage to collect a bill, unless the roommate agrees.

If you want the roommate out, you must work it out between you or talk to your landlord.

If the roommate's name is NOT on the lease, talk to the landlord. The landlord may be willing to lock your roommate out, BUT you must permit the roommate to take his or her stuff.

*7.41. Deposits and Multiple Roommates

If roommate A moves out and roommate B remains and gets new roommate C, what happens to the deposits? There is NO LAW on this, so it is up to the landlord. Check the lease first. If it says nothing, then usually the landlord either forfeits A's deposit for breaking the lease or tells A that A can get his or her deposit back when everyone moves out. Usually the landlord will require C to post a new deposit.

Sometimes the landlord tells A to get the deposit money directly from C, and the landlord will refund A's old deposit to C at the end of the lease.

Clear as mud? What you should really understand is that it is up to the landlord. You have no control over this. Be sure everyone understands what is going to happen.

Moving Out Early

If you have decided that you must move before your lease expires, be aware of the consequences. Although these sections are starred, they only apply to an oral lease if you fail to give a thirty-day notice of move-out or if your lease was for a specific period of time.

*7.42. Reasons for Breaking a Lease

Except for failure to make certain repairs, there is seldom a legal reason to break the lease. A roommate moving out, illness, loss of job, or quitting school DOES NOT give you a legal reason to move.

*7.43. Deposit or Cost of Reletting

Read your lease. Most leases have a clause that forfeits the deposit if you break the lease and move out early. Some leases have a cost-of-reletting charge. The amount of the cost-of-reletting charge may be more than your deposit. It will be charged if you break the lease. Your deposit will be deducted from it, and you will owe the remaining balance. Charges for cleaning and damage can be deducted from the deposit first. The remaining deposit is then deducted from the cost of the reletting fee, and you will owe the balance.

*7.44. Rent Owed

Breaking the lease also makes you liable for the rest of the rent due under the lease. If your lease ends May 31, but you move out on March 31, you owe the rent for April and May.

The landlord should make a reasonable attempt to re-rent the apartment. If he or she has a new tenant move in the first of May, then your lease is cancelled at that point. You owe rent only through April.

If the apartment remains vacant, in spite of the landlord's attempt to re-rent it, you owe rent for the remainder of your lease—in this example, April and May.

Will your apartment get re-rented right away? Consider these circumstances. Are there other empty apartments in your complex? The landlord does not have to rent your apartment first. If the complex is full, there's a better chance that your apartment will get rented quickly. Also consider what time of year it is. More people move at the end of May, end of August, and end of December. If you can time your move-out at one of those times, you increase the chances that your apartment will be rented quickly.

Give the landlord as much notice as you can that you will be moving out. This lets him or her know that your apartment will be available to rent. He or she may get it re-rented before you move out, then you won't owe any rent.

*7.45. Collection of Money Owed the Landlord

To collect rent and cost of reletting owed him or her for your early move out, the landlord can do any of the following:

1. Bill you repeatedly
2. Turn your name over to a collection agency and let the agency attempt to collect from you.

3. File the debt on your credit report, thereby giving you bad credit for seven years.
4. Report you as a lease-breaker to a business that keeps track of such tenants. This might make renting more difficult in the future if your new landlord checks your references with them. (*Note*: Not all cities have this type of business.)
5. Sue you in court.

*7.46. What Is the Landlord Likely to Do?

The greater the amount of money owed to the landlord, the more likely the landlord will pursue you for the money. So, if the landlord gets the apartment re-rented quickly and you owe him or her only $200, it is less likely that he or she will use all of the steps listed above.

*7.47. What If the Landlord Sues?

Many landlords do not sue because it costs them some money for filing fees and an attorney. The other reason the landlord may not sue is the difficulty of getting blood from a turnip. You're the turnip and the "blood" is money. In other words, the landlord may sue and win a judgment of not only the rent owed but also his or her attorney's fees and court costs; HOWEVER, the landlord may never be able to collect anything from you because you don't own anything.

Texas law allows a single person $30,000 worth of personal property ($60,000 if you are married) that cannot be seized to pay a judgment debt. Personal property is everything but land. For most young people, $30,000 covers everything they own.

Special Note: The $30,000 covers your car, furniture, clothing, and so forth, BUT it does NOT cover savings accounts, certificates of deposit, or large checking accounts. If your checking account just barely covers your monthly expenses, it is probably protected.

Because of this difficulty in collecting a judgment, many landlords choose not to sue. However, some landlords WILL SUE anyway, hoping, like you hope, that someday in the future you will have property.

*7.48. Are Your Parents Responsible?

Not if you were eighteen or older when you signed the lease AND your parents DID NOT cosign or guarantee the lease.

*7.49. Roommates

If one roommate moves out, the remaining roommate must pay the additional rent or find a new roommate. Failure to do so means the remaining roommate must move out, too. The landlord can pursue both of you for breaking the lease, EVEN THOUGH it is really the first roommate's fault. Legally, you are both responsible. This is not fair, but it is the law.

Special Note: For those of you thinking that it might be better to get evicted, read §§ 7.67–7.69 on eviction. The bottom line is that you still owe the rent, even if you are evicted.

Proper Move-Out Notice

Your lease expires in one month, or it has already expired, and you are living on a month-to-month basis, or you're on an oral lease that is month to month, and you want to move out legally. What do you do? Follow the steps below.

*7.50. Give Your Move-Out Notice

In most cases, this will be a thirty-day notice. If your lease says a different amount of time, follow the lease. If you're on an oral lease, you must give one rent-paying period's notice. Usually you pay rent monthly, so it will be a thirty-day notice, but if you pay rent every two weeks, then give two weeks' notice.

Give the notice in WRITING. This is required by most written leases. It is not required in an oral lease situation, but it is still the best way to go. Date the notice and keep a copy.

Under many written leases, you MUST give notice on the first of the month. If so, be sure it is on the first. Even if you don't pay your rent until the third, give your notice on the first. If you give it on the third, a picky landlord can say that he or she DID NOT get thirty FULL days' notice and refuse to refund your deposit.

If your lease does not specify notice on the first or if you are not on a written lease, you can give your notice on any day. You can give it on April 13 to move out on May 13. The landlord must then allow you to pay rent for only the first thirteen days of May.

Special Note: Remember, a notice to move out from one roommate is typically taken by the landlord as notice from all roommates. The landlord assumes everyone is moving out and will re-rent the apartment. If only one roommate is moving out and the remainder are staying or getting a new roommate, check with the landlord. Probably no notice of move-out is necessary because the apartment won't be vacated.

However, if one roommate gives notice and the landlord assumes that all of you are moving out and then re-rents the apartment, he or she can INSIST that you all move.

*7.51. Ask for Cleaning Instructions

Some landlords include them with the lease. Others hand them to you when you give your move-out notice. Still others have none. Generally speaking, cleaning means just that, including scrubbing handprints off walls, vacuuming out window sills, cleaning appliances, especially the oven, and shampooing the carpet. Some landlords also want all nail holes filled in.

7.52. Special Cleaning Fees in the Lease

Some landlords reserve a certain amount of your deposit for a "cleaning fee." Find out from the landlord what this fee is for. Sometimes, it is for carpet cleaning. If it is, you don't need to clean the carpet too. Sometimes it is just for "cleaning." It will be deducted, even if the apartment is spotless. It is legal to do so because you agreed to it when you signed the lease.

*7.53. Get the Landlord to Walk through with You

This way the landlord can point out anything that is not acceptable. You'll have another chance to clean it.

If the landlord can't or won't walk through with you, get a non-roommate friend to notice whether it is clean. If a dispute arises over cleaning, this friend can be a valuable witness in court.

*7.54. Damages Versus Normal Wear and Tear

The landlord cannot charge you for "normal wear and tear," but he or she can charge for damages. Sometimes it is hard to tell which is which.

If the carpet was new when you moved in three years ago and you have kept it clean with no stains, but it has begun to pack down in the traffic areas, that is normal wear and tear. You shouldn't be charged for it. If, on the other hand, you spilled red fingernail polish on it, that is damage, and you can be charged.

In case a dispute arises as to how serious the damage was, TAKE PICTURES for future use in court. Photographs can settle many arguments.

*7.55. Move-In Inventory 2

Remember this? I told you about it back in § 7.16 when I talked about moving in. Now it becomes valuable. Ideally, before the landlord charges you for any damage, he or she should check his or her copy of the move-in inventory and be sure the damage was not done by a previous tenant. If the landlord fails to do this and charges you for something already noted on the move-in inventory, then produce your copy of the move-in inventory and show your time/date stamped photos and point out the damage. I hope you kept your copy because this should resolve that charge.

* 7.56. Return All Keys Promptly

The landlord might be able to argue that you haven't really moved out until all keys are returned. You might end up owing several days of rent for however long you've kept the keys.

Some written leases have a specific charge for late key return.

* 7.57. Give the Landlord Your Forwarding Address

Until ALL roommates have done this, the thirty-day period (see § 7.59) for refund of the deposit DOES NOT start. All such addresses should be given IN WRITING.

* 7.58. Single Deposit Refund for Multiple Roommates

Check your lease. Some landlords reserve the right to make only one refund check and send it to one roommate. Sometimes they put all roommates' names on the check. Sometimes they put only one. Find out the landlord's policy. You want all roommates' names on the check, so that all of you must sign the check to cash it.

If you have a dishonest roommate who gets the check and signs your name to cash it, you can file felony forgery charges against him or her. Your complaint is against the roommate, NOT the landlord.

* 7.59. Deposit Refund

Once you have 1.) given proper move-out notice, 2.) cleaned, 3.) moved out, 4.) turned in keys, and 5.) given forwarding addresses of all tenants, the landlord has thirty days to refund your deposit. He or she must put in writing any deductions and the reasons for the deductions. Again, deductions can be made for inadequate cleaning and damage. Deductions cannot be made for normal wear and tear.

* 7.60. Disputes over Cleaning or Damages

When you get the itemized list of deductions, attempt to discuss any problems with the landlord. If this does not resolve the situation, you may then choose several courses of action against the landlord.

You can file a complaint with the BBB; the Texas Attorney General's Office for Consumer Affairs; the local apartment association, if your landlord is a member; a tenant association, if there is one in your town; the dispute resolution center, if your area has one; or file suit in small claims court. (Information about all of these courses of action is listed in chapter 8.)

If court is your choice, once in court, the burden is on the landlord to prove that his or her charges are reasonable. If you win, you are entitled to your court costs and attorney's fees.

In a dispute, your eyewitness who checked the apartment for you and any photographs you took can be of great value (§ 7.53).

* 7.61. No Refund or Itemized List after Thirty Days

First call the landlord to find out what the problem is. If this doesn't solve the problem, you can file suit against the landlord in small claims court. The landlord is presumed to be acting in bad faith if the refund or itemized list hasn't reached you within thirty days. You may then sue the landlord for three times the deposit plus one hundred dollars. If you win, you are entitled to your court costs and attorney's fees as well.

At trial, the landlord must show the court why he or she was late and that he or she was not acting in bad faith. If the judge or jury finds that the landlord did act in bad faith, no deductions can be made from the deposit for any cleaning or damage. You will be awarded three times the full amount of the deposit, plus one hundred dollars, plus attorney's fees and court costs.

If the landlord convinces the judge or jury that he or she had a good reason for being late with the itemized list or refund, then deductions can be made for lack of cleaning and damages, if the landlord proves such charges reasonable. Obviously, you get to dispute the charges to the judge. In this case, the most the court could award would be the full deposit, court costs, and attorney's fees. The landlord could countersue for additional amounts if claimed damages are more than the deposit.

The longer it has been past the thirty days, the harder it is for the landlord to show a good reason for being late.

True Story

Theresa Anyone finally moves out of her apartment when the lease is up. She gives proper move-out notice and turns in her keys; she cleaned and provided her forwarding address to the manager. She waits for her deposit refund.

Six months pass with no refund and no written explanation. Theresa calls the manager many times. Each time the manager assures Theresa that she will get her full deposit back in just a couple of weeks.

Finally, Theresa goes to the attorney for students. The attorney talks to the manager, but no money appears. The attorney advises Theresa to file suit in small claims court (see § 8.11) on her own without a lawyer. The filing fee is $65. Theresa sues for three times her $150 deposit ($450) plus $100 for a total of $550, as allowed by statute, since the deposit is now five months past due.

The hearing date is set. Theresa discovered that her old manager has hired a lawyer. In a panic, Theresa returns to the attorney for students. The attorney reassures Theresa that she can handle this case without a lawyer.

"I guarantee, Theresa," says the lawyer, "that you will know as much or more than her lawyer does about this statute. Here is a copy of it. Most lawyers seldom deal with this kind of case, because there is little money in it. All you have to prove is proper move-out procedure, that you gave your forwarding address, that it is past thirty days since you moved out, and you've received neither your deposit refund nor a written statement. You then explain why you sued for $550, and your job is finished. The manager must then explain to the court why she has waited so long to refund your money. If she doesn't have a good reason, the money is yours. It is very hard to come up with a good reason to withhold both the money and a written explanation for five months. If by some strange chance, the manager does convince the judge that she had a good reason, then you won't get the treble ("treble" means "three times") damages and extra $100. You still have a good chance of getting your basic deposit," says the attorney.

"You really think I can do it on my own?" asks Theresa.

"Yes, Theresa, you can do this. Come back after the hearing and let me know how it turns out," says the attorney.

"Okay," says Theresa.

After the hearing, a jubilant Theresa returns to the attorney for students.

"I won it all," she shouts. "It was just like you said. I proved my part. Her lawyer tried but couldn't get her to give a good reason for withholding my deposit. The judge awarded me all $550. When her lawyer asked the judge why he was awarding treble damages, it was obvious the lawyer didn't know about the law. I volunteered to show her lawyer my copy of the statute. It was great. And I got my court costs, too."

If Theresa Anyone can win a case like this, so can you.

Special Note: Remember, you have to have followed proper move-out procedure to use this statute. To look it up online yourself, it is "Texas Property Code §§ 92.101 to 92.109."

*7.62. Withholding Your Deposit from the Last Month's Rent

DON'T! The landlord can sue you for three times the wrongfully withheld rent; he or she will probably also end up winning court costs and attorney's fees too.

*7.63. Foreclosure

If the mortgage holder (legal owner of the property) has repossessed the apartment complex from your landlord, it is your old landlord who owes you a deposit refund, not the mortgage holder. You can sue your old landlord for the deposit, but the odds are that you'll never collect anything because he or she has no money.

Special Note: A new mortgage holder, after a foreclosure, can demand a new deposit from you, demand that you move out, giving you a thirty-day notice, or demand that you sign a new lease.

*7.64. Bankruptcy

If your landlord has filed for bankruptcy, you become a creditor of the landlord, just like everyone else they owe money to. It is your landlord who owes you the deposit. You should receive a Proof of Claim form from the bankruptcy court or trustee to file with the court. If you don't get such a form in the mail, contact the nearest federal bankruptcy court for the form. You can fill it out yourself. The filing is free and can be done by mail. The odds are not good that you will ever see your money, though.

*7.65. Sale of Property

If your apartment complex has been sold to a new owner by your old owner, voluntarily (not through bankruptcy or foreclosure), normally your old owner will transfer your deposit to the new owner, and it is the new owner who will refund your deposit. You are supposed to be notified by your old landlord, but he or she may forget.

There are some cases where deposits are not transferred to the new owner, and you must go back to the old owner for your money. You find this out from the new owner.

If the new and old owners are batting you back and forth like a ping-pong ball and none of the help agencies can resolve it, sue both landlords in one suit, and let the court resolve it.

Generally speaking, a new owner must honor any lease still in effect when the owner buys the property.

Eviction and Other Steps to Force You to Live Up to Your Lease or to Move Out

The most common reason for being evicted is nonpayment of rent. Most of the actions described in this section deal with that. However, you can be evicted for any "material" breach of the lease. This includes having noise complaints against you, violating the no-pets rule, having people not on the lease living in the apartment without the landlord's consent, and many other things. I'll indicate which paragraphs apply to eviction for reasons other than failure to pay rent.

*7.66. Notice on Your Door

This is a polite, or not so polite, note left by your landlord to remind you that you owe rent. Many landlords leave such a note as a first step. There is no requirement that this type of note be given.

*7.67. Lockout

Some landlords skip the polite note and go straight to a lockout. To lock you out, the landlord must first give you a warning letter—at least three days before locking you out—telling you the date that you will be locked out if you fail to pay your rent. If by the date stated in the letter you still have not paid, the landlord must leave a note on the door, telling you where you can get a key, twenty-four hours a day. When you go to get the key, the landlord can ask you why you haven't paid your rent. Regardless of whether you pay rent or not, the landlord MUST GIVE YOU THE KEY to get in. A lockout serves as a way to confront you, a way to talk to you eyeball to eyeball. This is NOT as a way to EVICT you. If you don't pay the rent due after you've been locked out once, you can be locked out again. In fact, you can be locked out each time you leave until you pay the rent. The landlord must always give you the key to get back in.

Landlords use this to confront you and annoy you so much that you'll pay the rent. If the landlord fails to let you into the apartment, you can:

1. Get a court order that allows you back in the apartment.
2. Recover from the landlord actual damages, one month's rent or $500, whichever is greater, attorney's fees and court costs, minus the late rent owed by you.

    Special Note: Any clause in the lease that says you give up this right is invalid.

*7.68. Eviction Notice

This must be in writing and give you three days to vacate (get out). A written lease may alter this time period. This notice must be delivered by mail, either first class or certified or delivered in person, to any person on the premises who is sixteen years old or older, or it may be left attached to the inside of the main entry door. The three days begin on the day that the notice is delivered. If you fail to move out, the landlord must file a suit for eviction.

*7.69. Suit for Eviction

The steps necessary to evict you through a court proceeding are outlined below. This lawsuit is called by the old common-law name of "forcible entry and detainer" or a "forcible detainer." It means a suit for eviction.

1. The landlord files the suit with the justice of the peace court asking for your eviction and any past-due rent.
2. You are served a copy of the papers by the sheriff's deputy or constable. The papers can be left with anyone sixteen years or older at your home. If unable to find you, the papers can be mailed to you or attached to your door.
3. You can move out at this time voluntarily and not go to the hearing. If you fail to appear at the hearing and the landlord sues for back rent, the landlord will win a judgment against you, awarding him or her the rent. Of course, he or she may win the judgment for back rent, even if you do appear.
4. The hearing date noted in the papers served will be no sooner than six days and no more than ten days from the date notice of suit is served. The hearing will be in front of the judge alone, unless you request a jury trial. To have a jury trial, you must request one, paying the jury fee of five dollars within five days of when you are served.
5. At the hearing, the landlord will tell his or her story first, explaining how you violated the lease. You tell your story

next. The judge or jury decides if you are in violation of the lease and if you owe any back rent. If it is decided that you broke the lease, the judge will issue a judgment against you.

6. The judgment gives you five days to leave the apartment with all of your property (except for items held by the landlord under the landlord's lien for back rent).

7. At the end of five days, if you have not left, the judge will issue a WRIT OF POSSESSION. This WRIT empowers the sheriff's deputy or constable to REMOVE YOU from the apartment, physically if necessary. If you won't remove your property, the landlord will, under the deputy's or constable's supervision. The items removed can be set outside but not on a public sidewalk or street and not in rain, sleet, or snow. The landlord CANNOT BE REQUIRED TO STORE your property. The deputy or constable can hire a warehouseman to remove and store your property AT YOUR EXPENSE.

    Special Note: If the landlord does store your property removed under a writ of possession, he or she can hold it HOSTAGE, until you pay back rent and storage fees, if so stated in your lease. All of the property can be held HOS-TAGE, because it was NOT seized under the special land-lord's lien.

8. Judgment in the justice of the peace court can be appealed to the county court or the county court-at-law for a NEW TRIAL by filing an appeal bond with the justice court within five days of the hearing. You will need an attorney for this.

*7.70. Eviction for Public Indecency Conviction

If you use the apartment for prostitution, promotion of prostitu-tion, display of obscenity, sale or distribution of obscene material to a minor, sexual performance by a minor, or if you possess or promote child pornography, and you are convicted of one of those offenses and all of your appeals of the conviction are abandoned or exhausted, you can be EVICTED. The landlord must still give you ten days' notice to move, regardless of rules of eviction in your lease.

*7.71. Abandonment of the Apartment

The landlord is entitled to assume you have abandoned the apartment if most of your possessions are gone and you do not sleep in the apartment for a reasonable time. Some leases say the apartment will be presumed abandoned if you are gone more than five days without informing the landlord of your whereabouts, if you have removed most of your property.

Abandonment lets the landlord go in and gather up any remaining possessions, store them, and get the apartment ready to re-rent, even if your rent is paid up to the end of the month. If you intend to return to get the remaining items and clean up, TELL THE LANDLORD. Otherwise, you may have to pay for any cleaning the landlord has done.

The landlord can hold abandoned items HOSTAGE for back rent and maybe for storage fees. Check your lease.

Chapter 8

HOW TO DO IT YOURSELF

Let's face it. There will be bumps in the road of your life. We all have them. The proof of your character is how you handle them. Standing up and facing adversity is the action of an adult. Because you are young, you will face many "firsts." First time being pulled over by the police, buying a car or hiring an attorney. The first time being treated like, and expected to act like, a grown-up.

This chapter deals with ways you may handle some of the glitches, and/or firsts, *all on your own*. I have gathered together some information on helpful agencies that are available to you. Some are free of charge; others are not. I have also added some aids in making complaints, that your voice may be heard, explained how small claims court works and, if those bumps in the road are bigger than you can handle on your own, how to find and get help from an expert.

Special Note: The following sections on how to make a complaint against a police officer also include making a complaint against a sheriff's deputy or highway patrolman. The words "officer" or "police officer" are used interchangeably for all three entities.

Complaint Against a Police Officer

We began chapter 3 discussing YOUR responsibilities at a traffic stop or when dealing with a police officer. You pulled over and stayed polite. You kept in mind the officer has a stressful and difficult job. You held your tongue and stayed courteous even if the officer was not and now you feel as if you want to file a complaint, so let's talk about it.

In my life and career, I have met and know hundreds of police officers. The great majority of them, I know, have chosen their career to serve their community with the upmost integrity. But I watch the news, and I read the newspaper. There are some bad ones, and I will be the first to say, they must be scouted out and some even put behind bars. President Theodore Roosevelt once said, "No man is above the law and no man is below it: nor do we ask any man's permission when we require him to obey it." Just like me and you, police officers are required to obey the law. I know it is difficult, and maybe even scary, when you think an officer you are dealing with is one of the bad ones. That is why I encourage you, when in contact with an officer, to comply with his or her orders and complain to the proper authorities later. Comply now, complain later. COMPLY NOW! COMPLAIN LATER! Get it in your head.

If a situation with an officer does escalate, and you feel as if his or her words or actions were improper, you have the right to report it. If you feel as if your civil rights have been ignored, you have an obligation to report it. Bad cops must be reported and removed.

8.1. ASAP

Moments after the incident, or as soon as possible, you should write down what happened. Write with as much detail as possible, but don't exaggerate. I can't stress this enough: tell the truth. Remember, most police agencies have video and audio recordings of every civilian contact. More and more officers, these days, have a body worn camera that is recording exactly what they are seeing and exactly what they hear. If you lie about one part of the incident, you won't be found credible about any of it, and lying to a police officer, under many circumstances, may be a crime.

When you have finished writing about the incident, put it away for a day or two, and then read what you wrote. Your emotions should not play a role in this. If your writing doesn't make sense because you were too emotional when writing, write it again. Use your first draft to help you but remove the emotion. The authorities that will read it don't get to deal in emotion. They may feel sorry for you that your feelings were hurt, but it is not against the law for an officer to be stern. The law is black and white with very little gray area. The authority looking at your complaint will be looking for officers stepping over the line.

If you have a witness, or witnesses, whose story will corroborate yours, ask them to write their story too. Don't discuss what you will write before each of you write your stories. I say this for a couple of reasons. You will be able to compare the two (or more) versions later. When you do, sometimes seeing the incident from someone else's viewpoint will help. The second reason is something you should think about. If you and your witness's versions are *exactly* the same, it may be a bit strange. It may look like a setup. You write your version, and let your witness write theirs without your input.

Many police agencies will want you to write your complaint on their form. This is not a requirement and cannot be forced on you. If you choose to rewrite your complaint on their form that is fine, but don't think your concerns will not be looked into if you don't.

8.2. What to Include

Your written complaint should include specific information. Always include the time, date, and location of the incident. If you know the officer's name and badge number, add that too. Don't say he was tall and had short hair on the sides. They all do and that won't help. If you know why the police had reason to make the contact in the first place, list that as well.

The most important part is what the officer said or did. This is where you need to be as detailed as possible. Was he or she rude or abusive, or did he or she use excessive force? Detail, Detail, Detail. Remember from English class . . . who, what, when, where, and why? Cover them all.

Once you have read over your statement and feel it is what you want to say, sign, date, and add a phone number to it. Under your signature, you should print your name because I am sure your signature is like mine and nobody can read it. If you have witnesses, make sure they include the same information: signature, date, phone number, and printed name.

Special Note: Most police agencies will not investigate an allegation against an officer for a difference in opinion for a traffic citation (a ticket). This is what court is for. An excuse of "everyone was doing it" is not a *good* excuse.

True Story

Steven Anyone was running late for work again. As you know, he has had his share of tickets, but he has also been late for work twice this week and the boss is catching on. He can't afford to lose this job.

As Steven's luck goes, he gets pulled over.

As the officer approaches, Steven rolls down the window and asks, "What's the problem?"

The Officer explains he clocked him speeding and asks for his license and insurance.

Steven was mad. He knows he was speeding but also knew several cars had passed him as he went down the interstate. "Why me?" Steven asked angrily. "All these cars blowing by you right now, and you pick me. They are a greater risk to society than me," he continued. "WHY ME?"

The officer took a step forward and leaned on Steven's door, so he could look him right in the eye and asked, "Have you ever been fishing?"

Steven was caught off guard, considered the question, and said, "Of course I have, I live in Texas."

The officer responded, "Did you ever catch *all* the fish?"

Steven took his ticket and later a tail chewing from his boss.

8.3. File a Complaint of a Less Serious Violation (Rude Officer Scenario)

Once you have read over your version and the version of your witness(es), you will need to make copies. If all that is done, you are ready to file it with the police department. Each department varies on this, but typically, you will have thirty to sixty days to file your complaint. You may only have thirty, so don't wait until the time is almost up. Human nature tells us that, if it were that important, you would take care of it quickly. Plus, if this cop is one of the bad ones, he or she needs to be stopped as quickly as possible, so he or she doesn't do to someone else what has been done to you.

You have a couple of options here for filing a complaint on a less serious violation. You may read over your complaint, get your thoughts together, and go to the police department. You will ask to speak with the supervisor on duty. He or she will be another police officer. In smaller communities, he or she will have to come in off the street. It could be several minutes, so don't get upset about the time; you want your police, at least the good ones, to be out on the street working, don't you? Once the supervisor is there, you may share with him or her your thoughts and concerns, or you may simply turn in your complaint. It is up to you. If you want to just hand the supervisor your complaint, you may ask him or her to sign and date it and make you a copy, so you can prove it was turned in. If you decide to discuss it, stay honest and consistent with what you have written. Police officers, even if they are not trying to, can be intimidating. Don't exaggerate anything, but don't leave anything out. I really can't say this enough. Tell the truth!

If you discuss it, the supervisor may share why an officer may do or say a certain thing and why the officer may have acted as he or she did. Keep in mind this is only the supervisor's understanding of what happened because the supervisor typically wasn't there at the time of the original incident.

In my mind, the best way to file a complaint "of a less serious nature" is to send it certified mail, return receipt requested, to the department (see § 6.25 Certified Mail). Remember, return receipt will make sure you get notice the police department received it.

8.4. File a Complaint of a More Serious Crime or Violation of Your Rights

If you are dealing with something more serious, such as a civil rights violation or even an excessive force complaint, you may write your complaint, as in the section above, and follow the steps below, or you may need to make an appointment with an attorney. This is entirely up to you and depends on the violation that occurred. Remember, if you won't complain, who will? Do you want what was done to you to be done to someone else? If you decide to go to an attorney, take your written complaint and those of your witnesses. The attorney will read through them, ask some questions, and explain your options. Those options could include anything from a lawsuit to contacting the FBI.

8.5. The Investigation

Once your complaint is received by the local police department, an investigator will be assigned to the case. He or she will contact you to let you know that your complaint was received. The investigator will begin by comparing your statements to the audio/video recordings of the officer. If something more is needed from you, he or she will request you to come in and discuss the incident. This is your option and should be taken seriously. If you are found to be lying to the investigator, or in the complaint you filed, you may be charged with a crime. This is the Class B misdemeanor of making a false report to a police officer.

Whether you go in or not, the investigation may continue. Once complete, you should receive by mail the findings of the investigation. Most agencies will use classifications similar to the ones below:

SUSTAINED—The investigation disclosed *sufficient evidence to clearly prove* some or all of the allegations made by you in the complaint, and disciplinary action could result against the officer.

NOT SUSTAINED—The investigation *failed to discover sufficient evidence* to clearly prove or disprove the allegation(s) made.

EXONERATED—The investigation reveals that the acts did occur, but the *actions taken were justified, lawful, and proper*.

UNFOUNDED—The investigation indicated that the alleged act(s) *did not occur*.

If after you receive the final notice from the investigator, you may still contact an attorney or the FBI. If you want to contact the Federal Bureau of Investigation yourself, you may do so.

The Texas offices of the FBI are:

Dallas Field office
One Justice Way
Dallas, TX 75220
http://www.dallas.fbi.gov
(972) 559-5000

El Paso Field office
El Paso Federal Justice Center
660 South Mesa Hills Drive
El Paso, TX 79912
http://www.elpaso.fbi.gov
(915) 832-5000

Houston Field office
1 Justice Park Drive
Houston, TX 77292
http://www.houston.fbi.gov
(713) 693-5000

You do not have to live in one of these three cities to file a complaint with the FBI. Agents are assigned across the state.

Finding and Hiring an Attorney

8.6. Finding a Lawyer

Some situations arise in which you must hire a lawyer for your own best interest, even if you are trying to save money. I have tried to point out some of those situations in this book.

The best way to find a lawyer is to get a referral from a friend who has used the lawyer and been happy with services received. I would take a friend's referral with more caution if your friend merely knows the lawyer as a friend, relative, or guy that lives down the street.

Because not everyone will be able to get a referral from a friend, various referral services are available. Participation in referral services by lawyers is voluntary, so not all lawyers are listed. Prices and quality of services are not guaranteed.

The State Bar of Texas has a statewide referral service with a toll-free telephone number, (1-800) 252-9690; the website is https://www.texasbar.com. Tell the operator in what city or county you need a lawyer and for what type of legal problems. You will be given a name or multiple names. You may also get a thirty-minute consultation with an attorney for twenty dollars by calling the above number.

Some counties and larger cities have local lawyer referral services. Some are listed below. If you do not see one listed for your area, *if your area has one, you will find it online.* These services are free.

ARLINGTON
Arlington Bar Association
(817) 277-3113
http://arlingtonbarassociation.org/

AUSTIN
Austin Bar Association
(512) 472-0279
http://www.austinbar.org/

CORPUS CHRISTI
Corpus Christi County Bar Association
(316) 883-4022
http://www.countyoffice.org/tx-nueces-county-bar-association/

DALLAS
Dallas Bar Association
(214) 220-7400
http://www.dallasbar.org

EL PASO
El Paso Bar Association
(915) 532-7052
http://elpasobar.com

FORT WORTH
Tarrant County Bar Association
(817) 338-4092
http://tarrantbar.org

HOUSTON
Harris County Bar Association
(713) 236-8000
http://www.harriscountybar.com

SAN ANTONIO
Lawyer Referral Service
(210) 227-8822
https://www.sanantoniobar.org

Another option that is available is a board-certified attorney. Board certification means the attorney has chosen to take an extra test in his or her special field. Besides passing the test, the lawyer must have been practicing at least five years and must devote a large percentage of his or her practice to that specialty. It does guarantee you that the lawyer has a certain level of expertise in that specialty. However, many good attorneys never choose to take the extra test. If a lawyer does only bankruptcy, you don't want to waste time trying to hire him or her for a criminal case. In your online search, you should include "board certified."

8.7. Hiring a Lawyer

Interview several lawyers. Most lawyers do not charge for the first visit unless you hire them. Be sure to ask about a fee when you make the appointment. Compare prices, but more importantly, compare personalities. You want to hire a lawyer that you feel comfortable with, not someone you don't like. On simple cases, like traffic tickets, whether you like the lawyer may not matter. On a lengthier case, personality matters a great deal.

Don't hesitate to ask questions because you think it may make you appear dumb. Lawyers don't expect the non-lawyer to know everything. Sometimes lawyers forget to explain things. ALWAYS ASK.

While it is good to explain your case thoroughly and to ask questions, don't abuse the relationship. The only thing a lawyer has to sell is his or her time and knowledge. Be reasonable in your demands on them.

Understand how you will be charged and for what. Many times you'll be asked to sign a fee contract. Be sure you understand it before you sign.

8.8. Fees

There are various ways to charge for legal services. Listed below are the most common ways. The attorney will decide which type of fee is used.

1. Flat fee: For a set fee of maybe, $500 the attorney will represent you. Be sure you understand what's covered. Does it include representing you at trial?

2. Hourly fee: For so much per hour, say one hundred dollars, the attorney will represent you. This means that the attorney keeps track of the time used in every phone call, every talk with you or the lawyer for the other side, all time spent in research and in court. The hours can add up. To try to get a realistic idea of the final bill, ask the attorney to estimate the least amount of time that a case like yours would take. Then assume that your case may take more. Amounts per hour vary from lawyer to lawyer and town to town.

3. Contingent fee: You pay no fee unless you win the case. You'll be asked to sign a contract stating the percentage of the final judgment or settlement to which the lawyer is entitled. Percentages vary from 25 percent to 40 percent. Under some contracts, if you don't win, you pay expenses, such as court costs. In other contracts, you do not have to pay expenses, even if you lose. Contingent fees are most often used in accident cases, malpractice cases, and civil rights cases. This type of fee cannot be used in a criminal case.

8.9. When You Are Not Happy with Your Attorney

Most attorneys are honest, hardworking, know the law, and do the best possible job for you. Misunderstandings can occur with the best lawyers, and naturally some lawyers are simply incompetent.

If you are unhappy, set up a face-to-face meeting with your lawyer. If you can't get an appointment, write a letter requesting one, which you send by certified mail, return receipt requested.

If unable to resolve your dissatisfaction, you have the right to fire the attorney. You can do this yourself or hire a new attorney who will inform your old attorney that he or she is fired. Your old attorney will give your new attorney your file.

You may or may not be entitled to a refund on any money paid to the old attorney. If the old attorney has done some work for you, he or she is entitled to some money, even if you fire the attorney.

If you feel the attorney has acted wrongly, you can file a grievance with the local bar association grievance committee. Find out whom to contact by contacting any attorney, https://www.texasbar.com/

(search for the "Grievance & Ethics Information" page), or call (1-800) 204-2222. This is a free service and can be very effective. The website actually has a video you may watch to help you with the process.

If you have a serious legal malpractice case, you may choose to sue the attorney in court for damages. You must hire an attorney to do this.

8.10. Free Legal Representation

Free legal representation is provided in various ways. You usually must meet certain poverty guidelines to be entitled to this free representation.

For civil matters, you can get representation several ways. There are various legal aid offices either federally funded or funded through some other agency. To qualify for aid, you must meet the federal poverty guidelines. Because of limited time available, these offices must concentrate on the most serious cases, such as divorce and housing. You may qualify financially, but if you need to probate a will, these offices may not be able to help you. To locate these offices, check under "legal aid" in the phone directory, look online, or with the directory assistance operator.

Most communities have lawyers that do occasional work for free. This is called "pro bono" work, from the Latin phrase *pro bono publico*. It means "for the public good." Usually, you are referred to a lawyer for pro bono work by one of the agencies noted above. Pro bono work is almost always done through referral only. Don't expect to pick out an attorney's name at random and get him or her to represent you for free.

Small Claims Court

8.11. Not Quite Like on TV

Small claims court *is considered* the people's court. It is set up so that you can use it without hiring a lawyer. However, you can use a lawyer in small claims court if you choose. The judge of the court is the local justice of the peace, and the court is located in your county and sometimes in the county courthouse.

Things are kept simple. The judge's office has a form, called a "petition," that you fill out to file your case. You need the name and street address of the party you wish to sue. You must have a street address because the sheriff's office must serve a copy of the petition on the person you are suing. A post office box number won't work. The filing fee can be any amount up to $150. You can request in the petition that the other party has to reimburse you for these court costs, as well as the amount you are suing for if you win.

You can sue for any amount of money up to $10,000. You can only sue for money, not an object, like your TV that your roommate kept. You can sue for the value of the TV. Be prepared when you fill out the petition to briefly write the reason why you are suing. By that, I mean be prepared to say that you are suing for your wrongfully withheld $200 property deposit, rather than that you are suing for $200 with no explanation.

You will be notified about the hearing date. If you need to force witnesses to come to court, you can do so by asking the clerk of the court to help you to issue a subpoena. There is an additional charge for this. Ask for the subpoena well in advance of the hearing date, so the sheriff's office will have time to serve the subpoena on your witness.

Before the hearing, the respondent (the party you are suing) may contact you to settle out of court. If the offer is acceptable, take it. If you insist on going to court, there is always the possibility you might lose and get nothing. If you want to recover the filing fee, make that part of your settlement. You do not get the filing fee back from the court if you cancel the case.

Your hearing is really a trial. It will be a trial in front of the judge alone unless you or the respondent asks for a jury trial. There is a small jury fee (about five dollars). The jury will be made up of six people.

Normally, small claims court trials take place fairly quickly after you file, sometimes in as little as three weeks.

If you decide to hire a lawyer, do so at the beginning of your case or as soon as possible.

If you are representing yourself, make an outline or notes for yourself to help you present your case in a logical and brief fashion.

The judge will give you some help with procedure. Below are some basic rules to follow:

1. In selecting a jury, ask questions of the jury to find out if the jury members are unbiased and have average knowledge of the subject of the suit.

   Example 1: If you are suing your landlord, find out if any jurors are landlords. Such jurors might tend to side with the landlord. Find out if anyone is, or has ever been, a tenant. That juror might tend to side with you. Those that aren't either one may tend to favor neither side.

   Example 2: In a traffic accident case, find out if all jurors drive. A non-driver might not be a good juror.

2. You have the right to mark out the names of any three jurors. The respondent has the same right. The first six not struck out will be the jury.

3. If you are the plaintiff (the one suing), you go first. You may tell your side of the story yourself. You can use notes. When you finish, the respondent gets to ask you questions. That's called "cross-examination."

4. You present all of your side of the case before the respondent presents his or hers.

5. If you have witnesses other than yourself, you must ask them questions like a lawyer would. They cannot just tell their story without questions. The respondent gets to cross-examine them, too.

6. When you are finished with your side of the case, the respondent gets his or her turn. After the respondent testifies, you get to cross-examine the respondent and all of his or her witnesses.

7. After all testimony, the judge or jury makes the decision and announces the winner.

8. Either party can appeal the results to the county court for a new trial if he or she does so within ten days of the

judgment. If no appeal occurs within that time period, then the judgment is final.

9. If either party does not show up for the trial, the party that does show up wins by default.

10. You must have live witnesses. Sworn written statements are not usually admissible in court. That means you can't use them to help your case.

11. If suing for a traffic crash, written estimates of car repair are admissible. It is even better if the estimate is notarized, or you can testify that immediately before the accident, your car was worth $4,000 and immediately after, $3,361.50. Everyone knows that you just subtracted the estimate from the value, but that is one legal way to present the evidence. You can do this even though you are not a mechanic. You can use photographs. It is not required, but it is better to have the person who took the photographs in court to testify about when and where they were taken.

12. If you need to sue for more than $10,000, you must file in a higher court. This means you must hire an attorney.

True Story

This story has nothing to do with small claims court, but it is too funny to leave out.

Let's visit Theresa Anyone one last time. Theresa goes to see the attorney for students. She is mad. Her ex-boyfriend, Lincoln, has been telling all of their mutual friends terrible things about her. She wants him stopped.

She says to the attorney, "How do I file a suit for DEFECATION of character?"

She is extremely puzzled when the attorney bursts out laughing. If you aren't laughing by this time, go look up "defecation." You undoubtedly would recognize this bodily function by another name.

8.12. Collecting on a Small-Claims-Court Judgment

The trial is the easy part. Getting your money can be the hard part, especially if you are dealing with an individual, like your ex-roommate. It is easier to collect from businesses, but there is no guarantee you'll ever collect. The court DOES NOT help you collect.

Under Texas law, an individual is entitled to have $30,000 worth of personal property (everything but land) exempt from being taken to pay a judgment debt. For a married person, the amount is $60,000. There is no garnishment of wages in Texas, except for court-ordered child support. A judgment lien can be placed against land, but the Homestead Act prevents you from forcing a sale of the land if it is a homestead.

The bottom line is that it can be very difficult to collect on a judgment from the average individual. Remember, the personal property exemption of $30,000 covers cars, tools of a trade, furniture, and various personal effects.

Savings accounts, certificates of deposit, stocks and bonds, and goods in excess of $30,000 for a single person or $60,000 for a married person are NOT protected. Any excess in a checking account, over and above reasonable living expenses, can be reached as well. However, a specific legal process must be followed. It takes a lawyer to do this. For the collection of small debts, this is not practical (see [3] below).

Businesses and corporations are usually easier to collect from, especially if they own land.

Since it is so hard to collect, why file in small claims court? Because the debtor you are suing may not know how hard it can be to collect from him or her, and therefore, he or she may pay once the judgment is granted. If he or she does not voluntarily pay, you can take the following steps:

1. *Writ of execution*: You pay a hefty fee to the sheriff's office, and a deputy will go out and demand the money. If the person refuses to pay, the deputy CAN DO NOTHING. This

is a bluff on your part. Generally, it is a waste of money because the debtor knows the officer can do nothing.

2. *Abstract of judgment*: For a small fee, you can get a certified copy of the judgment from the justice of the peace court and file it with the county clerk for another small fee. This puts a lien against any land owned by the debtor in THAT COUNTY. If you know of land owned in another county, you can file the certified judgment there too. The lien will attach.

   As noted earlier, if the land is a homestead (main residence), your lien probably won't do any good because homesteads are protected.

   There is one advantage to filing the abstract, even if you know it cannot be attached to any land. Credit-reporting agencies usually record any abstract of judgments against the debtor's credit. Wishing to clear up a black mark on credit has caused many debts to be paid.

3. *Hire a lawyer*: This is expensive and therefore not practical for small debts. For a fee, a lawyer will send post-judgment interrogatories. These are questions about what property the debtor owns and where it is. The interrogatories must be answered under oath (before a notary). Failure to do so can result in punishment by the court.

The interrogatories are only worth the cost if the debtor really does own property that is not exempt from seizure. You may or may not know whether this is likely. Remember, you pay for the lawyer's services whether you recover any money on the judgment or not.

Voting

It is no secret that the United States has one of the lowest voter turnouts of all industrialized countries. For a country so fiercely protective of our freedoms, the fact is surprising that we don't exercise this right that is denied to so many others around the world. In my mind, voting is not just a right but one of our most basic civic duties. Voting gives each of us a voice in specific issues and, maybe more importantly, those chosen to govern us. Communities with higher voter turnout also have greater access to candidates and elected officials, thus granting those citizens more say in decisions that affect their community, as well as our state and our country. Candidates and elected officials simply respond more often to neighborhoods (at the local level) and communities (at the state and national level) where more people are registered to vote and actually do vote. Think about it! Those seeking office are less likely to visit or listen to people or communities that don't participate in elections.

8.13. If You Don't Vote

If eligible and you chose not to vote, you are allowing others to decide who is elected and what issues matter. Also, keep in mind that there are some in our country that can't vote because of their age or because they are not yet citizens. Your vote may represent their voices too. Sometimes those who are unable to vote or choose not to vote are the ones affected most by the government or other social services funded by government, for example, education, public safety, or even health care.

8.14. If You Are Not Registered, You Can't Vote

To vote in Texas, you must be registered. If you want to register you may pick up a voter registration application at any government office, your DMV (Driver License Office), or most libraries, or you may download one from the website of the Texas Secretary of State at: www.votetexas.gov. Once you have completed the application, you may mail or drop off the application to the voter registrar in your county. In most smaller communities, that is your local tax assessor's office (where you get your license plates for your vehicle). If you are unsure, you may use the website of the Secretary of State to verify the registrar's location for your county. Once the application is accepted your voter registration will be effective thirty days from registration.

8.15. Eligibility to Register to Vote

You are eligible to register to vote if:

You are a United States citizen;
- You are a resident of the county where you submit the application;
- You are at least eighteen years old on Election Day;
- You are not a convicted felon (you may be eligible to vote if you have completed your sentence, probation, and parole);
- And you have not been declared by a court exercising probate jurisdiction to be either totally mentally incapacitated or partially mentally incapacitated without the right to vote.

8.16. Where, When, and How to Vote

Once the application has been approved, you will be mailed your voter registration card with your name, address, and the number of the precinct where you will be able to vote. (A precinct is a certain geographic area in your county where you live.) Your county's website will publish the address for your polling place for your precinct. Your local newspaper will also publish the addresses on the Saturday before Election Day. Once you find out where you are going, you should arrive between 7 a.m. and 7 p.m. to cast your ballot on Election day. Early voting is the seventeenth day through the fourth day before Election Day. Early voting is usually 8 a.m. to 5 p.m., Monday through Friday.

Special Note: As I write this section, a new court battle has begun here in Texas. This challenge to the current law may change a few of the acceptable forms of photo identification requirements listed below. Remember, this list is according to the law on the books as I write. You may need to do a little outside research when you are ready to vote. Use votetexas.gov to verify.

8.17. Acceptable Forms of Photo ID

In order to vote in Texas, not only must you be registered to vote but also you must possess and present one of the following acceptable forms of photo identification:

- Texas driver's license issued by the Texas Department of Public Safety (DPS);
- Texas Election Identification Certificate issued by DPS (see Special Notes 1–3 below);
- Texas personal identification card (ID) issued by DPS;
- Texas license to carry a handgun issued by DPS;
- United States military identification card containing the person's photograph;
- United States citizenship certificate containing the person's photograph;
- or United States passport.

With exception to the US citizenship certificate, the identification must be current or have expired no more than four years before being presented for voter qualification at the polling place.

Special Note 1: Texas Election Identification Certificate (EIC) is a form of identification used only for voting purposes. The EIC is valid for six years. You may apply for an EIC at no charge, but if you already have one of the other forms listed above, you are not eligible for an EIC. You can apply at any Texas Department of Public Safety office (Driver License Office) by filling out an application. This application—form DL-14C or Spanish form DL-14CS—can also be downloaded from www.dps.texas.gov.

To qualify for an EIC, you must provide to DPS:

- Documentation to verify you are a US citizen;
- Documentation to verify your identity;
- Your valid voter registration card (or a voter registration application);
- Documentation to show that you are a Texas resident;

- And documentation to show that you are at least seventeen years and ten months old or older.

The information, such as name and date of birth, on all the documents you submit, must match. If the name is different on the documents, then you must provide documentation that verifies a legal name change, for example, a marriage license, a revised birth certificate, or a court-ordered name change. Documents must be original or certified copies. Photocopies will NOT be accepted.

Special Note 2: Fingerprints are NOT taken and a warrant check is NOT conducted when applying for an EIC.

Special Note 3: An EIC will NOT be accepted by DPS to verify identity when applying for a Texas driver's license or Texas ID.

8.18. Supporting Forms of ID

If you do not have one of the acceptable forms of photo identification listed in § 8.17 and you cannot obtain one for any legitimate reason, you may request, fill out, and present to the election clerk at your polling place a "supporting form of identification" (listed below). You will also have to fill out and file a form called a "Reasonable Impediment Declaration." On this form, you will explain why you are unable to obtain an acceptable form of photo identification and state you are the same person as listed on one of the following:

- Certified birth certificate (must be an original);
- Copy of or an original current utility bill;
- Copy of or an original bank statement;
- Copy of or an original government check;
- Copy of or an original paycheck;
- Or copy of or an original government document with your name and address (an original is only accepted if the document has a photograph attached).

Special Note: A *reasonable impediment* includes things like lack of transportation, disability or illness, lack of birth certificate or other documents needed to obtain acceptable photo ID, work schedule, family responsibilities, lost or stolen photo ID, or photo ID applied for but not received. You may also describe another reasonable impediment you have on the form.

8.19. Exemptions for Not Presenting an Acceptable Form of Photo ID

If you are a voter with a "consistent" religious objection to being photographed or you do not have any form of the acceptable photo identification listed in § 8.17 due to a natural disaster that was declared by the president of the United States or by the governor of Texas, you may vote on a provisional ballot. You must then appear at the voter registrar's office within six days after Election Day and sign an affidavit swearing to the religious objection or natural disaster for your ballot to be counted.

Another exception is if you have a disability and do not have one of the acceptable photo identification listed in § 8.17. If so, you may file for a "permanent exemption." This is done with your county voter registrar. You must include documentation from either the US Social Security Administration as evidence you have been determined to have a disability, or from the US Department of Veterans Affairs proving your disability rating to be as least 50 percent. This will allow you to vote and not provide any other documentation.

Special Note 1: If you need assistance while at your polling place, you may be assisted by a person of your choice or an election worker to read the ballot or sections of the ballot to you aloud. The person must take an oath that he or she will not try to influence your vote, will mark your ballot as you direct, and will not tell anyone how you voted. If you do not speak English or only communicate by sign language, you may select anyone—other than your employer, an agent of your employer, or a union representative—to help you communicate with election officials.

Special Note 2: If you are physically unable to enter the polling place, an election officer will bring your ballot to you at the entrance of the polling place or to your car at curbside. If you are going alone and will not be physically able to enter the polling place, it would be wise to call ahead to the voter registrar.

8.20. Work as a Student Election Clerk

If you are at least sixteen years old, a US citizen, and enrolled in a public, private, or home-school program, you can participate in our Texas electoral process by serving as an election clerk. After completing any required election worker training program, you will be able to work at a polling place during early voting and or on Election Day. You must have consent from your principal and written permission from your parent or guardian to serve.

Not only will you be paid an hourly wage but the experience of serving your community and state can be rewarding, not to mention how good it looks on a résumé or college application. Plus, if your school requires community service each year, it will work for that too.

Working under the supervision of the election judge, you may assist with distributing ballots, making sure only qualified voters are permitted to vote, and answering voter's questions and explaining the use of voting equipment.

If you are interested in this program, you will need to contact your local voter registrar and fill out the "Student Election Clerk Application and Permission Slip."

Your school district may excuse you for the purpose of serving as an election clerk for a maximum of two days in a school year. Remember, the polls are open until 5 p.m. and Election Day is on Saturday for most elections.

Purchase of a Vehicle

Let's switch gears a little and talk about something that can be great fun. New vehicles are fun to drive and fun to own and very exciting but can be frightening when buying one on your own. Let's cover the ins and outs.

This section is not intended to be a detailed statement on the law of contracts. It is intended to alert you to some basic laws governing contracts for the purchase of a vehicle and other areas for concern.

8.21. The Contract

You have an absolute right to have a copy. Be sure to read the contract before signing. Be certain all blanks are filled in. If any alterations are made to the printed form, all parties should initial the changes.

8.22. Three-Day Right to Cancel the Contract

There isn't one. On certain consumer contracts, a three-day right to cancel exists. The purchase of a car IS NOT one of them. Once you've signed, you have a binding contract.

8.23. Cosigning

A cosigner is equally responsible for making payments on the car with the first signer. This is true even though the cosigner does not have the payment book or possession of the car. If the first signer fails to pay (defaults), then the creditor can look to the cosigner for payment.

Special Note: The creditor seldom notifies a cosigner before repossession, acceleration of the note, and demand for payment in full is made. If you cosign a note or have one cosigned for you, keep in touch with each other to avoid this problem.

8.24. Acceleration of Note

Almost all sale contracts have an acceleration clause. This clause permits the creditor to demand payment in full if you default on the note in any way. This includes late payments. It is far better to pay on time, but if you cannot, contact the creditor to explain. Many creditors will permit late payments if they are not *too* late and you have gotten permission. However, almost all contracts contain a statement that says that the creditor retains the right to declare a default for a late payment or other violation, even if the creditor has previously allowed late payments. In other words, the creditor can change his or her mind and without notice to you. In some situations, the car might even be repossessed, without notice, after the second late payment.

8.25. Insurance

The instrument that binds you to the purchase (sales contract and/or secured note) always has a clause that requires that you keep the car fully insured for the length of the loan. This is not "credit life insurance," which is optional, but regular comprehensive car insurance to cover you if you are involved in an accident. This is NOT liability only, but full coverage. The creditor wants to make sure the car is paid for if it is wrecked.

If you purchase comprehensive insurance, your insurer will automatically notify the creditor that you have done so. If you don't purchase insurance, the creditor gets no notice. This will trigger the creditor's purchase of its own insurance.

The creditor's policy covers only repairs to your car (not personal injuries or damage to the other car). The cost of this policy will be added to the note on the car. This may be done without advance notice to you. This type of creditor's policy DOES NOT meet the State of Texas requirement of liability insurance that you must present to an officer when pulled over.

8.26. When to Insure a New Car

You should insure the car at once before you drive the car off the lot. The title does NOT have to be in your name or even properly signed for you to purchase insurance. Call your insurance company when you decide to buy.

8.27. Leasing instead of Owning

It has become popular to sign a long-term lease contract for a car instead of buying. The lease is usually for twenty-four, thirty-six, or forty-eight months. The actual lease contract is lengthy and resembles a purchase contract. Generally speaking, it requires you to carry comprehensive insurance. It also requires that you pay for mechanical repairs. In fact, you have all of the duties and responsibilities of an owner, but you don't own the car.

The potential problem in this area is in attempting to BREAK THE CONTRACT. Most people know you can't break a purchase contract, but they think a lease contract is different and not as binding. IT IS NOT DIFFERENT. Even if you voluntarily turn the car in, you still owe the remainder of the contract price. It works like a repossession. The creditor will sell the car and apply the money received to the debt. This is seldom enough to pay off the debt in full. You still owe the remainder.

Remember, a lease contract is just as binding as a sales contract.

8.28. Deposit

If you are required to pay one, remember, in most cases you don't get it back. If you buy the vehicle, it is credited to the purchase price. If you DON'T BUY, the seller gets to KEEP IT, as payment for having held the vehicle off the market for you and for having turned away other buyers. Be sure you understand what happens to the deposit before you pay it.

8.29. New Cars

All new cars are covered by a warranty for a set period of time or set number of miles. A written explanation of the warranty should accompany your sales contract. Be sure you understand how to use the warranty. The main limitation in a warranty, besides the time and mileage limits, is that you must use a dealership for repairs.

8.30. Lemon Law

All new cars purchased after October 1, 1983, are covered under the Texas Lemon Law.

If the same problem has been repaired four or more times by the dealer within the express warranty term or during the period of two years following the date of delivery to the purchaser, whichever is earlier, and the problem still exists;

  OR

the vehicle is out of service for repair for a cumulative total of thirty or more days during that two-year period,

  and

the defect substantially impairs the use and market value of the vehicle,

  and

the manufacturer or distributor has been notified of the defect IN WRITING and has been given an opportunity to repair it, the Texas Lemon Law applies.

You must request a hearing before the Texas Motor Vehicle Commission in writing, providing a copy of the letter sent to the manufacturer or distributor within six months of the expiration of the express warranty or eighteen months after the purchase of the vehicle, whichever comes first.

The commission telephone numbers and website are:

(512) 465-3000
Toll-free (1-888) 368-4689
www.txdmv.gov.

The commission will hold a hearing to determine if you have met all of the requirements of the law. If you have done so, the commission will order the manufacturer to provide a new car or refund the purchase price of your car minus a reasonable allowance for your use of the vehicle.

If you are unhappy with the decision of the commission, you may sue the manufacturer at your own expense.

Be sure to keep all of your work orders for car repairs so that you can prove how many times the car has been worked on.

Special Note: The Lemon Law applies only to NEW CARS. Even though the manufacturer's warranty transfers to a second owner, if it has not expired, the Lemon Law does not. The second owner has bought a "used" vehicle.

8.31. Used Cars

BUYER BEWARE is the watchword here. You can get a real bargain in a used car if you take simple precautions. You can buy a real headache if you do not.

The general rule is that used merchandise (including vehicles) is sold "as is." Theoretically, the seller is supposed to warn you of known defects. However, it is very difficult to prove that a seller knew of a particular defect before the sale. Unless the seller expressly warranties the vehicle, the seller has no responsibility for any repairs. Any such warranty should be in writing.

The seller must not make any misrepresentations about the condition of the vehicle. If you ask specific questions, the seller must answer. A direct lie, if it can be proved, can invalidate the contract. A statement of "I don't know" is difficult to prove as a lie in most cases. It is very difficult to break such a contract based on oral misrepresentations.

The safest and most IMPORTANT thing to do is to take the used car to a mechanic of your choice and have him or her examine it before you buy. There may be a fee for this. A mechanic cannot spot all defects, but he or she can spot most major ones. The payment of the fee is worth it, if it saves you from a bad purchase. If the seller will not let you take the car to your own mechanic, DO NOT BUY THE CAR.

If the seller is an individual, ask to see the title to the car before you pay any money. This should be a "clear title," that is, with no lienholder. In some instances, you can purchase a car with a title that has a lienholder, usually a bank, but the car can be sold only with the lienholder's permission. The lienholder may want payment directly from you to ensure that the note gets paid off before releasing the title.

Note: The lienholder MUST give the released title to the seller of the car, whom you must trust to sign it over to you. If the seller will give you "power of attorney," which you show the lienholder, the lienholder can send the title directly to you.

8.32. Non-negotiable Title

This is stated on the face of the title if you are still paying on the car. This "title" cannot transfer ownership. Negotiable means sellable. Your creditor (lienholder) who holds the note on the car also holds the negotiable title. When the note and any other charges are paid in full, the negotiable title will be mailed to you by your creditor. In the place on the title where the lienholder's name is given, the word released with the date will be written. This title is now "negotiable," and you can use it to sell the car.

If you want to get a new title, with the lienholder's name removed, you may do so. To file for a new title, turn in the old one and pay a small fee at the tax assessor's office in the courthouse. In about six weeks, you'll receive the new negotiable title through the mail. Remember, a new title without the lienholder's name is optional.

8.33. Negotiable Title

This title will show your name as the current owner, your permanent address, and information to identify the car. The lienholder line will be blank. A previous owner's name will be listed if there was one. There is also a signature line for you to sign on the face (front) of the title. DO THIS AT ONCE. That signature will be used for comparison when you sign on the back to sell the car.

8.34. To Sell or Buy a Car

The car seller must have "clear title" (that means no lienholder). If you are buying from an individual, ask to see this. If the seller doesn't have the title, DON'T BUY THE CAR. (This is usually not a problem with dealers.)

It is no longer necessary to sign the title before a notary public, even though the title may still have the place for the notary to sign on its back.

8.35. Getting the Buyer's Name on the Title

The buyer's name and permanent address must be filled in on the back of the old title above the seller's signature on the negotiable title. Take this to the county tax assessor's office (usually found in the county courthouse). As buyer, you will also have to fill in a new title application form stating the purchase price. The sales tax will then be assessed based on this price. You must sign this form under oath. There is a place for the seller's signature on the new title application form, but a signature is not mandatory.

In six weeks to two months, the new title will come to you in the mail. If you buy from a dealer, the dealer will do all of this for you.

As the buyer, you should transfer the title into your name IMMEDIATELY AFTER PURCHASE. DO THIS FOR TWO REASONS:

1. The license tag renewal is mailed to the address on the title. If the title has not been reissued in your name, the reminder goes to the old owner, not to you. You may forget to renew the tags until a police officer reminds you.
2. You will find out if the seller has properly signed the title right away, before the seller disappears. If you wait to transfer the title for six months, you may discover that the title is unsigned and have no way to contact the old owner. You then DO NOT HAVE TITLE TO THE CAR.

True Story

If you haven't noticed, trouble seems to run in the Anyone family. Trey Anyone loves his brother's motorcycle so well that he decides to buy one for himself. He finds an ad in the paper and pays cash for a used motorcycle. Cindy Seller gives Trey the title.

Trey has learned from Steven's mistakes. The motorcycle is registered, inspected, and insured before Trey ever rides it. Trey has also gotten his license endorsed for a motorcycle. However, he forgets one major thing. He neglects to turn in the title, pay the sales tax, and get a new title in his name. Six months later, the license tags are about to expire. Trey realizes he must find the title to be able to get the new sticker for the tags.

The title is lost. He can't find it anywhere. The tax assessor's office tells him that the last registered owner is the only one who can file for a lost title. Trey has no idea of how to reach the old owner. He can't remember the name. When he returns to the address, the old owner has moved. The new tenants know nothing about the old owner. Trey returns to the tax office. They run a check on the motorcycle's license number and give Trey the old owner's name and the address that was on the title. It is the same address that Trey has already tried. He tries Google and even a Facebook search, but the old owner, Ms. Seller, has disappeared.

When the tags expire, Trey can no longer ride his motorcycle. What can he do? As a last resort, Trey mails a letter to Ms. Seller at the old address, hoping that the post office will forward it to some new address. Trey gets lucky. The letter is forwarded, and Ms. Seller calls Trey.

For once, the Anyone family has a happy ending. This entire hassle could have been avoided if Trey had filed the title right away.

8.36. Repossession

All installment sales contracts allow repossession for failure to follow the contract. In Texas, NO NOTICE is required before repossession. As noted in the earlier paragraph on ACCELERATION OF THE NOTE, a late payment, not previously approved by the lender, can result in repossession and payment in full being due at once. This is true even if the lender has allowed previous late payments.

8.37. Do Not Keep the Certificate of Title in the Car

If the car is stolen, it will allow the thief to forge your name and sell it. Keep the title in a safe place where you keep other important papers.

8.38. Odometer

This is the device that measures mileage on a motor vehicle. Texas law now requires that a sworn odometer statement be made by every seller in a car sale. On new title certificates there is a section on the back specifically for this. If no such section is on your title, there is a separate form for this, obtainable at the tax office at the county courthouse or online. A completed form, either the separate one or the one on the title itself, must be sworn to by the owner and turned in with the old title at the time of the new title application.

Special Note: It is no longer necessary to swear before a notary, BUT you are still swearing. If you lie, you can be prosecuted for perjury.

It is illegal to roll back the odometer to read fewer miles than the vehicle has actually been driven. This crime is punishable as follows:

First offense: jail time not exceeding two years and/or a fine up to $1,000

Second offense: confinement in jail for not less than thirty days nor more than two years and a fine no greater than $2,000.

If you find evidence that this has been done to a car you have purchased, you should report it to the State Department of Motor Vehicles or the district attorney for the filing of criminal charges. You may also have a separate civil action under the Deceptive Trade Practices Act. Seek your own attorney for the civil action or file a complaint with the Texas Attorney General's Office for Consumer Affairs.

Registration and Inspection

8.39. Registration (License Plates)

In Texas you are required to renew your license plates once a year. The month in which you must renew will be the month in which you purchase a new car or, in the case of a used car, the month already noted on the car's windshield sticker. Usually, the state will send a reminder to the name and address on the certificate of title a month before renewal is due. However, failure to receive a notice is NOT A LEGAL EXCUSE for driving with expired plates. If you fail to get a notice and fail to contact the local tax assessor's office for renewal, you will get a TICKET with a fine of up to $200.

Normally, renewal means paying a fee that varies with the weight of your car and receiving a new sticker to place on the car windshield. If you receive the notice by mail, you can renew by mail. You can also renew in person at the county tax assessor's office.

A few years ago, the law on inspection stickers changed. A sticker is no longer required to be displayed on the windshield with the Registration. Your vehicle will still have to be inspected before it can be registered each year. Gas stations, oil and lube stations, and garages will prominently display a red, white, and blue sign with a map of the State of Texas on it if they do inspections. The fee for the sticker and inspection is usually about $15, and the inspection takes only a few minutes. If any repairs need to be made, there will be an additional charge. If the vehicle passes inspection, you will be provided with an inspection report that states your vehicle passed and can be registered by the local tax assessor. If the registration is due, the tax assessor's office will get notice on their computer system also that the vehicle passed inspection. Repairs to bring the car in compliance with state law *must* be completed before the car can be registered or issued a sticker. Tires, brakes, lights, horns, mirrors, windshield wipers, front seat belts, steering, wheel assembly, and exhaust and emission systems must all be inspected.

The state gives you a five-day grace period. That means if your registration sticker was due in November, you may get it registered up until December 5th. Beginning on December 6, you will be ticketed. The ticket carries a fine of up to $200. If you do receive a ticket and your registration has been out for less than sixty days. Get the registration updated and provide proof to the court. Most courts will dismiss the charge with only a $20 dismissal fee.

Special Note: If you replace your windshield, don't forget to get a new registration sticker. The old sticker CANNOT be transferred from the old windshield to the new windshield.

8.40. Number of Plates

Texas law requires that all Texas cars have a front and rear license plate and that the rear plate be lighted at night. Failure to meet either of these requirements can result in a ticket being issued that subjects you to a fine up to $200. If you have a little sports car with no front license plate bracket, go ahead and drill the holes in the bumper. A license plate in the front window will not get you out of the ticket.

8.41. Temporary License Plate

These are the cardboard plates on new vehicles bought from dealers. They are good for only twenty days. You should receive your metal plates within that time period. If you do not, contact the dealer at once. If you are caught driving with temporary plates after the twenty-day period, you can be ticketed and fined up to $200. Failure to receive the metal plates is not a legal excuse.

It is ILLEGAL to transfer the plates from one vehicle to another vehicle. They are registered to a specific vehicle.

Car Repair

After you have had the crash, now comes one of the most frustrating parts of life you may experience . . . car repair. Below are a few tips on how to avoid trouble and what you may do if trouble occurs in spite of your best efforts.

8.42. Seek Out a Good Mechanic

A reliable mechanic is worth his or her weight in gold. If you find one, tell your friends about him or her so maybe he or she will stay in business. How do you find a good one? Ask friends and relations.

When you have picked out a garage, check it out BEFORE you use it. Call the local Better Business Bureau (BBB) (see § 8.62) to see if they have had any unresolved complaints on the garage. If you live in a city that has a Texas Attorney General's Office for Consumer Affairs, you can also check with them. It's a good sign when there are no unresolved complaints. However, if the garage is a new business, there may not have been time for complaints yet.

Match your car to the mechanic. If you have an unusual foreign car, you may not want to use "Joe Blow Mechanic." You don't want him learning about the car by working on it.

Special Note 1: If your car is still under warranty, you must use a dealer for the warranty to be in effect.

Special Note 2: If you have had your car repaired by a mechanic who guarantees his or her work, you must return the car to him or her if the problem recurs. If you are out of town, call the mechanic for instructions. Failure to do so may cancel your warranty.

8.43. Get a Written Estimate

If you want to know the cost of repair ahead of time, get an estimate of repair from the mechanic before you start. Be clear on whether the estimate is just a guess or is the actual cost. If the estimate is to be the actual cost, it is a binding estimate. Get the mechanic to write "binding" on the estimate.

Make it clear that you must be called to approve any additions to the estimate. On the work order estimate itself, have the mechanic note the duty to call you for additional work.

8.44. Work Order

Sometimes you may get an estimate several days or weeks before you are going to have the work done. If so, you will be asked to sign a "work order" when you bring the car in for work. Your signature authorizes the work. Be sure to keep your estimate, AND be sure everything on the estimate gets transferred to the work order. If you are going to have the work done the day you get the estimate, the estimate will probably be done on the work order itself. As noted above, be sure to get the notation "binding estimate" and "call before any additional work" WRITTEN on the work order.

8.45. Do Not Let Work Be Done on Your Car without a Written Work Order

You have no way to prove agreed prices or approved work. If the mechanic won't write up a work order, DON'T LET HIM OR HER WORK ON YOUR CAR.

8.46. Ask for the Replaced Parts Back

This can be valuable evidence of what work was actually done. You must ask for these BEFORE work is done on your car to be sure of getting the parts. Keep them for a while to be sure the repair is okay. It is best to put this request in writing on the work order.

A few parts are always returned to the maker and so will not be returned to you.

8.47. New or Used Parts

To save money, it is sometimes possible to use a rebuilt or a used part rather than a new one. Be sure you and the mechanic are clear on which is to be installed. Rebuilt parts almost always have a warranty or guarantee for a set period of time. Used parts may or may not have this protection. All warranties or guarantees must be in writing.

8.48. Don't Leave Property in the Car

Most garages have signs posted saying the garage is not responsible for items left in the car. This is correct. If you must leave the car overnight, find out where the car will be kept. The mechanic is responsible for damage or theft only if he or she is negligent in some fashion.

True Story

Steven's car needs repair. He takes it in for repair. He sees the sign that says the owner is not responsible for articles left in the car. Steven carefully removes his baseball equipment, school books, coat, and anything else that was loose in the car. He must leave the car several days.

When he goes to pick it up, he discovers that someone has ripped the in-dash stereo out. This is an old car, and Steven does not carry vandalism insurance on it. He goes to the garage owner. After all, the car was in the owner's custody. The owner refuses to pay for the damage and points to the sign about articles left in the car. Steven looks at him in disbelief.

"This wasn't 'left' in the car. It was part of the car," Steven says. The garage owner just shrugs.

Steven sues the garage owner in small claims court. He wins but never collects his money before the garage owner files for bankruptcy.

None of this was really Steven's fault. This time he could not have avoided the problem. Chalk it up to the first of my rules to live by: "Life is not fair."

8.49. Warranties

This is a guarantee of free replacement or repair for a set period of time. Warranties can be on many different things.

Some examples are:

1. New car warranty: For a set number of miles or specific period of time (see § 8.29 on new car purchases for more details).
2. Extended warranty: This is an optional feature that you can buy when you buy a new car. Extended warranties vary greatly in length, cost, and coverage.
3. Parts warranty: New parts and rebuilt parts usually have a warranty for a set period of time.

4. Warranty of labor: The mechanic may warrant or guarantee his or her work (parts and labor) for a set period of time.

Special Note: Get all warranties in WRITING. A verbal guarantee is next to impossible to prove.

8.50. Save All Paperwork

It is vital to have all receipts, work orders, estimates, and warranties for proof if you later need to question what was done or not done.

8.51. Unauthorized Work

Upon arrival to pick up your car, you discover that work you DID NOT authorize was done. The mechanic failed to call you. TECHNI-CALLY, you don't have to pay for the extra work, BUT the mechanic can remove whatever parts were used in the unauthorized work and put your old ones back on. In other words, he or she doesn't get to benefit from unauthorized work, BUT neither do you. Often it is impractical or impossible to have the mechanic undo the work. You may have to pay under protest and follow the steps in § 8.54.

8.52. Higher Charges

You authorized all of the work, but the cost is higher than you were told. If you have "binding estimate" noted in writing, you have the law on your side. Keep calm and try to reason with the mechanic. Most cases of higher charges occur on estimates that were not binding. If "binding" is not written on the estimate, you may have to pay.

8.53. What Can You Do?

Stay calm and polite. It is very difficult to get people to do what you want if you are screaming at them. The mechanic's instinctive response is to scream back and stick to his or her guns. Calmness and politeness should correct the problem if it is simply an error.

If the mechanic says it is no error and reasoning with him or her fails, go over his or her head to an owner or manager. If this fails, READ ON.

8.54. Pay under Protest

If you want your car back, you will have to pay to get your car. A MECHANIC'S LIEN allows the mechanic to hold the car until you pay. You may note in the memo area on your check the words "under protest."

8.55. Do Not Stop Payment on the Check

In some circumstances, this is a crime. You don't want to wake up to sheriff's deputies on your doorstep at 6 a.m. with a warrant for your ARREST! In some circumstances, it isn't a crime, BUT this is a technical point. You'd need a lawyer to figure out the difference. It is not worth the risk of going to jail.

8.56. Mechanics Lien

Not only can the mechanic hold your car until you pay, but if he or she releases the car to you and your check bounces, is returned because payment is stopped, or the account is closed, HE OR SHE CAN RETAKE YOUR CAR. He or she can't take it out of a locked garage, but he or she can take it from almost any place else. This doesn't happen very often, but it can happen. The mechanic can hold it until you pay.

8.57. Complain to Better Business Bureau or the Attorney General's Office

These agencies require a written statement setting forth the problem with the mechanic in full detail. Once filed, these agencies contact the mechanic for a response. They will attempt to negotiate an acceptable settlement of the issue. They both work in the spirit of cooperation. Neither agency can force the mechanic to do what you want, but they are frequently successful anyway. Filing is free. You may file with either one or both agencies. The BBB is listed in the business pages of your phone book. The attorney general's offices are listed in this book in § 8.63. Contact the one nearest you.

8.58. Dispute Resolution Center

See § 8.62 and § 8.64 for more information. These services may be able to resolve your problem.

8.59. File Suit

You can do this yourself in small claims court for amounts up to $10,000. A lawyer is not required. For a higher amount you must go to a higher court with a lawyer.

You may be able to sue under the Deceptive Trade Practices Act for three times the amount, in certain cases. For this kind of suit, you need a lawyer.

8.60. Dissatisfaction with the Work

If the problem comes back, take the car back. The mechanic should fix it. If the same problem occurs again, you may want to take the car to another mechanic for an opinion. If you suspect work was not done that you were charged for, take the car to another mechanic with the work order and returned parts. He or she may be able to tell you if work was done at all OR if work was improperly done.

Get the second mechanic's opinion in writing. Go back to the first mechanic and attempt to reason with him or her. If this doesn't work, follow all of the steps noted above for DISPUTED BILLS.

How many times must you allow the first mechanic to repair the same problem? Probably several. If it is still not fixed, take the car to a second mechanic.

You can try to insist that the first mechanic PAY for the second mechanic to fix the problem, but it may not work. In that case, you must just pay the second mechanic yourself and sue the first one.

8.61. Leaving the Car with the Mechanic

Whether you leave it because you don't have the money to pay an undisputed bill or you leave it because you are disputing the bill, DON'T leave it for several months. The mechanic can charge you reasonable storage fees at a daily rate. When the bill plus storage fees equals the value of the car, THE MECHANIC CAN SELL THE CAR.

Reporting Agencies

8.62. Better Business Bureau (BBB)

This is a private, nonprofit agency that helps promote good business practices. Files are kept on BBB members and on any businesses that have had a complaint filed against them. BBB services are free. Use them for two purposes:

1. Check out the business BEFORE you use it. If you're taking your class ring to the jewelers to be cleaned, check out the jeweler BEFORE you leave the ring. The BBB will have information about any previous unresolved complaints. It doesn't guarantee that you'll be satisfied, of course, but at least you avoid known problems. You may do this by phone.
2. AFTER a problem occurs, complain about a problem with a business in writing. The BBB will contact the merchant and attempt to resolve the situation. The BBB works in a spirit of cooperation and cannot compel a business to act. However, most reputable businesses do not want an unresolved complaint report against them at the BBB. That means the business has an incentive to work something out with you.

If the BBB does not resolve the situation to your satisfaction, you can sue in small claims court (see § 8.11). If you look up the BBB online but make sure you are checking the BBB that represents the area where you live.

Consumer Affairs

8.63. Texas Attorney General's Office for Consumer Affairs (A.G.'s Office)

Branch offices are located in seven Texas cities, whose addresses are listed below.

Make a written complaint to the A.G.'s Office. It can be the same complaint letter you send to the BBB. A letter will be sent to the merchant you have complained about. The A.G.'s Office will attempt to resolve the complaint. If unsuccessful, you still have the right to sue.

The A.G.'s Office specializes in violations of the Texas Deceptive Trade Practices Act, but the A.G.'s Office will accept complaints on other matters.

If enough unresolved complaints are filed with the A.G.'s Office, they can seek an injunction on behalf of the people of Texas to stop the practice. They have also been successful in reaching out-of-court settlements on problems that affect a large number of consumers.

This service is free. Offices are located in the many cities. If there is not one located in your town or city, file with the closest office. Go to www.texasattorneygeneral.gov/ and click on "Consumer Protection" on the top banner. You also have the option of filling out a printable form and mailing it to the Austin office.

Office of the Attorney General
Consumer Protection Division
PO Box 12548
Austin, TX 78711-2548
(512) 463-2185

8.64. Alternative Dispute Resolution Center

Some cities have available a private, nonprofit, nonjudicial mediation service that attempts to resolve complaints through the use of trained mediators. You file the complaint and the agency sets up a meeting between you, the trained mediator, and the other party. The mediator helps you reach a solution acceptable to all parties.

This system also works on the spirit of cooperation. The agency cannot compel the merchant to participate, but many will. The agency cannot enforce the decision, but mediation frequently works. If it does not, you can still go to court.

Sometimes there is a small charge, and sometimes the service is free. Not all areas have such a service, but more are being created every day. Do an online search for "Dispute Resolution" in your area.

Vacations and Spring Break

If traveling outside of our state, be sure you remember the laws vary from state to state. A lot of young people travel to Mexico for their spring break or senior trip. Read the following to be smart and as safe as possible.

8.65. Entering and Traveling in Mexico

Visiting Mexico can be great fun, but BE CAREFUL. You are subject to all Mexican laws, just like a native Mexican. You want to have a good time, not end up a victim of a crime or in jail for breaking the law. PLAY IT SAFE. Stay in groups. Do not go off alone. If you drink, moderate your drinking. Good judgment is lost with too much alcohol consumption.

If you are only crossing for a few hours to a border town, Mexican customs does not require you to have a passport or visa. Do have some form of picture identification. If you intend to stay longer, you need a passport, birth certificate, voter registration card, or affidavit to prove that you are a US citizen. It is best to carry one of those items anyway to avoid any problem in returning to the United States. If you are a permanent resident alien of the United States and wish to stay more than a few hours in Mexico, you must show your US permanent residence card. If you are in the United States on any other visa, contact the nearest Mexican Consulate for visa information. The following cities have consulates:

Austin	(512) 478-2866
Brownsville	(956) 542-4431
Corpus Christi	(361) 882-3375
Dallas	(214) 932-8670
Del Rio	(830) 775-2352
Eagle Pass	(830) 773-9255
El Paso	(915) 533-3644
Houston	(713) 271-6800
Laredo	(956) 723-6369
Midland	(915) 687-2334
San Antonio	(210) 227-9145

Special Note: It is illegal to carry firearms or explosives into Mexico.

8.66. Driving Your Car in Mexico

American insurance policies DO NOT cover driving in Mexico. DO NOT drive in Mexico, for even a day, without insurance coverage of some sort, because an ACCIDENT IN MEXICO IS A CRIMINAL OFFENSE. It is likely you will be taken from the scene of the accident directly to the POLICE DEPARTMENT for the amount of DAMAGES to be estimated. If you are judged at fault in the accident, your car is impounded and you can be detained. To be released you must pay cash or have MEXICAN INSURANCE. Therefore, it is best to buy Mexican insurance before you cross the border. The cost is quite reasonable. A policy can be purchased for a single day. For information on Mexican auto insurance, contact an insurance agency that sells Mexican auto coverage. Such agencies are most commonly located in Texas border cities, although you may be able to locate such agencies in all major Texas cities.

If you are traveling more than twenty-five kilometers (15.5 miles) beyond the Mexican checkpoint, you must carry proof of car ownership with you. A certificate of title or a notarized affidavit of ownership is acceptable to Mexican customs. The Mexican insurance company can help provide the affidavit of ownership.

Remember, if you go past the twenty-five-kilometer limit, you also need proof of US citizenship.

8.67. Bringing Items Back from Mexico

If you buy items in Mexico, you should know that certain products CANNOT be brought into the United States and will be confiscated by US Customs with no reimbursement to you. PROHIBITED ITEMS include products made from lizard, snake, crocodile, and sea turtle; ivory; furs of certain species, including jaguar, leopard, tiger, ocelot, margay, tiger cat, seal, and polar bears; most feathers and live birds; many plants, fruits, vegetables, and some meat. Naturally, ILLEGAL DRUGS are also prohibited. You cannot import PETS, lottery tickets, liquor-filled candy, or FIREARMS or AMMUNITION. You cannot mail alcoholic beverages.

DUTY-FREE ITEMS YOU CAN BRING BACK: One hundred cigars, 200 cigarettes, and one liter (33.8 fluid ounces) of wine, beer, or liquor can be brought in, if you are twenty-one years of age. You may also bring back $400 worth of goods not on the prohibited list. REMEMBER, US CUSTOMS DOES NOT HAVE A SENSE OF HUMOR. NO JOKES! Contact your nearest US Customs office for more information.

8.68. Returning from Mexico

To return to the United States you must pass through US Customs. If you are a US citizen, you must have a photo ID with your picture on it AND a birth certificate OR a United States passport.

Special Note (for noncitizens): If you are a permanent resident alien be prepared to show your permanent resident visa. If you are a nonresident, you must present a valid passport with a valid visa. If you are on a student visa, you must show a valid I-20 form ("Certificate of Eligibility for Nonimmigrant Student Status") showing enrollment in your college or university. Failure to do so may cause REENTRY INTO THE UNITED STATES TO BE DENIED! To enter Mexico, contact the nearest Mexican Consulate for information.

Go forth and be a responsible Texan.
—Judge Cypert

INDEX

Federal Bureau of Investigation (FBI). *See* complaint against police officer: contacting the FBI

felonies. *See* crimes

finding an apartment, 152

fines: cursing the police, 38–39; expired inspection sticker, 217; expired license tags, 217; expired temporary license tags, 218; failure to appear, 43; failure to call police to accident, 57; fake or altered license, 21; leaving the scene of accident, 56; license suspension, 17–19; no driver's license, 17; no proof of insurance, 19, 37; odometer, rolling back, 216; paying to get out of jail, 78–79; traffic tickets, 44. *See also* crimes

fingerprints, 76

free legal representation: civil, 196; criminal, 84

gifts: dating couples, 119; engagement rings, 126; wedding gifts, 126. *See also* property

Graduated Driver License Program, 9–16; intermediate license, 11; learner's permit, 9–10; provisional license, 11; Texas Driver's Education Course, 11–12; time requirements, 9; unrestricted license, 9, 11. *See also* Texas Driver's Education Course

graffiti, 86–87

guns. *See* handguns

handcuffs, 76

handguns, 99; illegally loaning, 100; license, 99; places prohibited, 100; when you may possess, 100

harassment: by bill collectors, 137; crimes, 90, 116; sexual harassment, 134

hazing, 88–89

health spas, 142–143

heroin, 104

HUD, 153

indecent exposure, 87

insurance, car: collision, 30; deductible, 28; fire, theft, and vandalism, 30; high or assigned risk plan, 32–33; how much coverage, 27–28; how to find insurance, 26–27; if you don't call police to accident, 58–59; if you drive someone else's car, 31; if you lend your car, 31; if you rent a car, 31; liability insurance, 28–29; loan agreement, 30; medical insurance, 30; minimum required by law, 27; not covered in Mexico, 31; personal injury protection (PIP), 30, 65; policy exclusions, 31; policy limits, 15, 68; premiums, 28; proof of insurance, 37; requirement of full insurance on new cars, 209; set rate plan, 32; State Board of Insurance, 33; Texas insurance plan, 32–33; types of coverage, 28–31; types of insurance policy, 209; underinsured motorist coverage, 29; unlicensed driver not covered, 31; use of car in a business, 31; what coverage is right for you, 30–31; when to insure your car, 209

insurance, proof of, 37

insurance, property, 161–162

intermediate license, 11

jail: holding cell, 76–77; how long you can be held after bond posted, 78; how to get out, 78–82; phone call, 76; what really happens in jail, 76–78